LEAD

OUT LOUD

KEYS TO UNLOCK YOUR PROFESSIONAL EXCELLENCE

Vincent Ivan Phipps, M.A.,

Certified Speaking Professional (CSP)

Printed in the United States of America

2nd Edition
ISBN 9780985138059

Communication VIP (Very Important People-skills)
Chattanooga, TN 37404

Cover Design: William Connell
Owner, Unified Tech
www.myunifiedtech.com

Connect with Vincent

Receive FREE newsletter, special rates, and other updates.

www.communicationvip.com

E-mail Vincent today to claim your Digital Copy!

Vincent@CommunicationVIP.com

What People Are Saying About Lead Out Loud...

Vincent has done it again! He has taken his high-energy personality and translated it into a masterpiece. Lead Out Loud provides key skills for new leaders to seasoned leaders in their industry. It takes the complicated and turns into simple baby steps of success for enhancing your leadership. If you want to elevate to the next level in leading others, this is the book for you.

Valoria V. Armstrong
President
Tennessee American Water

Once our organization received training on the 'Four Types of Questions' in Chapter 4 of Vincent's book, I saw a substantial positive impact related to communicating with both current and potential clients. Asking the right questions and listening effectively has led to a better understanding of our client's needs, stronger partnerships, and increased value delivery.

Jonathon Bullard
President - Zeco & Zee Company
The Vincit Group

Lead Out Loud is a gift to anyone who wants to succeed in life. The book is full of insights and captivating antidotes that can be used throughout life. Vincent Ivan Phipps inspires you to reach your fullest potential.

Beverly Moultrie, CEO, B³HR

Vincent Phipps has a passion for helping people discover their leadership style. This book will empower you to communicate and listen effectively. These are essential qualities every leader must cultivate to be successful.

David Banks, Ph.D.
Member of National Speakers Association
President of Noble Success LLC

About the Author

Vincent Ivan Phipps is an expert in amplifying attitudes and communication excellence. He is the owner of Communication VIP Training. The VIP represents the company's expertise, Very Important People-skills. The VIP also are Vincent's initials! As a motivational speaker, facilitator and speech coach, Vincent has spoken in over 400 American cities and foreign countries. Within three years, Vincent endured the following tragedies: breaking his neck in an almost fatal car accident, leaving his corporate job after 13 years, and he and his wife suffering the loss of their son, Maxton Victor Phipps (he was their MVP). During these times of struggle, Vincent developed strategies to channel negative energy towards positive outcomes. He parlayed these skills into techniques for personal and professional empowerment. Vincent has been speaking professionally for over 20 years. He is the author of Lead Out Loud: Keys to Unlock Your Professional Excellence! Vincent has an undergraduate degree in Speech/Language Communication and a Master's in Leadership/Management. Vincent is the recipient of the highest earned honor awarded by the National Speakers Association, the CSP, Certified Speaking Professional. Since 1973, only 12% of the world's best speakers and trainers have been recognized to receiving this international speaking designation. Vincent is also a retired, undefeated, national storytelling champion. Out of the top 500 ghost story tellers in North America, Vincent was ranked 8th in the nation by TripAdvisor.

Introduction

At one point I pondered, "What kind of parents would give their child the initials, 'VIP', surely rendering them to a life of having to constantly exceed expectations?" I am now proud to carry the initials with the great honor of continual recognition of their sacrifices to enable me to have a chance at an awesome life! My grandfather's name is Vaughn Phipps. My father's name is also Vaughn Phipps. My older brother's name is Vaugh Ian Phipps. Giving him the initials, VIP. My parents named me, Vincent Ivan Phipps. My mother told me she selected the name, Vincent" because it meant "Conquering one". She chose Ivan, "Gift from God". My company name of, Communication VIP Training and Coaching, has a dual meaning in the VIP. Foremost, the VIP represents what we teach, "Very Important People-skills". This is the foundation upon which effective communication is built.

Our son, became our family's MVP, as we named him, Maxton Victor Phipps. Phipps men are never late to any event. Our son, in keeping with tradition, unfortunately, was born fifteen weeks prematurely on December 25, 2011, and passed away within minutes of his birth.

Whether in tragedy or in triumph, we all must choose how we respond to each moment in our lives. When reading this book, use these approaches to give yourself the fuel and the tools to make better decisions whether inspiring others, communicating, handling conflict, leading key people, or presenting valuable information.

Don't wait to communicate!
Don't quiet your quest.
Lead Out Loud!"

Chapter 1:
The Spit-Shined Mindset -
Amplify Your Attitude

Lead Out Loud!

How do You Define, Attitude?

Attitude Is the Outlook You Choose.

What is the cost of a bad attitude? Just how much is lost on poor customer service due to lacking the right fuel or tools?

While serving as President of the Tennessee Chapter of the National Speakers Association; a hotel hosting one of our meetings misspelled our greeting on their marquee. I asked the front desk attendant for assistance. The attendant called the hotel manager. When the manager arrived, the two of them began debating who was at fault. The hotel maintenance man arrived and grabbed a ladder and fixed the sign to properly say "welcome" instead of "melcome." The front desk attendant and the manager were so entranced in the argument that neither noticed the correction of the problem. When I thanked the maintenance man for being proactive and fixing the problem, he simply smiled and said, "You're' m*elcome*!"

If someone were to tell you, "She's got an attitude!" or if someone said to you, "I don't like your attitude," the word "attitude is often used in negative connotations. Having an attitude implies negativity, sarcasm, or an overall unpleasant disposition. Attitude may have various implications or definitions.

Although it is humbling to be perceived as a person with a persistent positive outlook, I, like anyone else, have challenging moments. When someone asks me, "How do you stay so positive? How do keep such a healthy attitude?" My answer is always the same. I tell them, "I choose." When they ask, "Choose? Is that it?" I say, "Yes, I choose to be happy over unhappy. I choose to be pleasant over unpleasant. I choose to be respectful over disrespectful. The situation may be out of my control. My attitude in that situation is 100%, up to me. I choose."

Attitude

When you think of the word, "attitude what words come to mind: perspective, disposition, approach? What do you think of when you hear the words, "an attitude": negative, pessimistic, sarcastic, difficult? It is intriguing that we can correlate emotions with words. One of my favorite topics to teach and train other on is attitude. In my two decades of being a communication consultant and trainer, attitude is the topic I feel is the most important yet where we receive the least amount of training.

Previously, I defined "attitude as choosing your disposition. I developed this definition when I first went skydiving. After teaching the basics of skydiving, my flight instructor, Reed the Rocket, asked if I had questions. I was so excited about getting on the plane to jump; I forgot to ask anything! Upon take off, my attitude was at its peak of positivity. When the plane's door opened, I looked out and became terrified, but it was too late. My instructor, me, and my now negative attitude were hurtling toward the Earth from 11,000 feet at over 200 miles per hour! I promptly began hollering and slobbering. Reed calmly asked me, "We are going to be falling for another few minutes. How long are you going to be hollering?"

It was at that moment I realized Reed and I were in the same situation. I chose to be scared and unsure. Reed chose to be calm and confident. Attitude is choosing your disposition.

Our attitudes may resist change. Instead of becoming mauled by change, become a motivator of change. This is accomplished by taking accountability for your goals and being proactive.

T.I.G.H.T.

To best set an attitude goal of change, remember to keep it T.I.G.H.T.

T	**Timed**	Set your goal for three dates: a start date, a checkpoint date, and a completion date.
I	**Informed**	Include numbers: dates, times, amounts, and percentages.
G	**Genuine**	Make a goal you want for your edification and fulfillment.
H	**Hard**	Make it challenging to establish a sense of accomplishment.
T	**Targeted**	Make it specific to you and your ambitions.

Let's say you wanted to save money or lose weight. Look at examples on the following pages of poorly developed attitude goals that will fall to pieces and those that are T.I.G.H.T.

Lead Out Loud!

Saving money	Loose Attitude Goal	T.I.G.H.T. Attitude Goal
	Try to save more money	**Have $10,000 in 200 Days**
Timed	Put away extra cash when I can.	June 1 – September 30
Informed	Save a few dollars each week.	$50/day for 200 consecutive days
Genuine	I will do the best I can.	This money will be my home deposit.
Hard	Try to remember.	Make a checklist to review weekly.
Targeted	I have been told I should do this.	I want to do this for my next home.

Losing weight	Loose Attitude Goal	T.I.G.H.T. Attitude Goal
	Get in better shape	Drop body fat to 25%
Timed	Exercise when I get more time.	January 1 – March 31
Informed	Look better in my clothes.	Lose at least 10 pounds.
Genuine	I want my friends to notice.	I want to fasten my high school jeans.
Hard	Walk a little bit every day.	Burn at least 500 calories an hour.
Targeted	Get respect from others.	Wear my swimsuit this Summer.

My friend Kyle always aspired to work on a pit crew for NASCAR. I accepted his invitation to attend a race at Bristol Speedway. While traveling on a dirt road near Bristol, TN, Kyle's truck caught a flat. This was before GPS was fully developed and my flip phone had no signal. It was dark, and I was getting concerned. Kyle pulls over. He clutches the steering wheel firmly. I think he is about to tell us we are stranded! He keeps his eyes on the wheel and asks me, "Can you take out your stopwatch?" Nervously, I say yes, hoping he knows how long it will take a wrecker or rescue service to find us. He yells, "Go!" jumps out of the truck in the pitch black. I hear a series of mechanical noises and what sounds like drilling. Kyle pops back into the truck with a childlike look of accomplishment. He turns to me and asks, "how long?" I look at the stopwatch and reply, "Two minutes and twelve seconds." Kyle exclaims, "Not my personal best but not too bad considering I couldn't see." Kyle starts the truck and safely drives on toward our destination.

Although we may be unable to choose our situations, we can control our situational attitudes.

CHAPTER CHALLENGE

During your next moment of challenge, release what you are unable to control and focus on what you can positively change

Chapter 2:
Know Your Spit -
Discover Your Leadership
Quotient

Lead Out Loud!

Leadership is less about a title and more about tenacity. Leadership is the tenacity to continuously adapt to ensure that a group of people can focus on a single goal. The most effective leaders can adapt to connect with those who choose to follow. Subordinates may follow managers and supervisors because of authority. We all have the freedom to choose which leaders we follow. This chapter will show you how to adapt to those who choose to follow you. This chapter will also provide the tools to help you establish rapport with key people. The goals for this chapter are:

1. Understand the traits of all four personality styles.
2. Learn the communication strengths and weaknesses.
3. Adapt to the communication "do's" and "don'ts."

If you are a skilled adaptor, you will usually have a better life, a better career, and be a better person. If you cannot adapt, it is going to be ugly. If you cannot adapt, your life will be limited. I want your life to be limitless. If you have not had a history of behavioral science, let me share this with you as an overview. My background is in Speech and Language Communication. I have also been a professor at the University of Tennessee, in Chattanooga (also referred to as UTC). I have written six books. I have three degrees and six certifications. However, none of that makes any difference if I cannot help you learn the skills to improve how you lead others.

I am a slow learner; I need things broken down to me in almost childlike simplicity. I have gotten over being embarrassed by asking, "Can you say that part again?" or "May I ask a question to ensure I understand?" Sometimes I need things spoon fed to me. I always need to read the information at least twice. I assume that everybody learns as slow as I do.

Fancy Word	Real-world definition
Behavioral Science	Study of how people communicate based on their personalities.
Interpersonal Communication	The disposition or approach a person has as it relates to people skills.
Introvert	A person who is soft-spoken and cautious to decide.
Extrovert	A person who is outspoken and quick to decide.
Task-oriented	A person who interacts with others for a result instead of a relationship.
People-oriented	A person who values other people's feelings instead of only the facts.
Pure Style	A person who has only one of the four styles as their primary style.
Blended Style	A person who has two styles as their primary style.
Tri-blend	A person who has three styles as their primary style.

If you do not have any idea about behavioral science, that is a fancy way of saying people skills. Make sense? My grandmother called it home training. What we are looking at is how to treat people, and how to adapt to them.

I grew up in Chattanooga, Tennessee. Chattanooga is the nucleus of what is nationally referred to as, "The Bible Belt." This phrase identifies an area of the Southeastern and Southwestern regions of the United States that have their ideologies influenced by the Christian Bible. In this Bible scripture, "*Do to others as you would have them do to you*" is found in the Book of Luke, Chapter 6 verse 31. This scripture is called "The Golden Rule." When it comes to honesty and integrity, the Golden Rule works well to treat others as you would want to be treated.

My great lesson on integrity occurred when I was ten. I had a perfect report card with perfect attendance. My father treated me to a 20-piece Chicken McNuggets. Usually, I received a box of *nine,* or I would have to share a box of 20 with my brother. This time, I would have the entire 20 McNuggets to myself. My father drove us through the drive-through. My McNuggets came in a cardboard box. I could feel that greasy, warm McNugget heat permeating through that thin box. The aroma of deep-fried chicken parts tantalized my nostrils! My father did not like food being eaten in his car, but I could not resist. I opened the box and counting each of my McNuggets. To my delight, they gave me an extra McNugget. There was a total of 21 McNuggets. Oh, happy day!

I held up that 21st McNugget as if I was offering a precious element as a gift to the Greek Gods. My father asked me, "Son, what are you doing?" I replied, "Drive Dad. They messed up. We got an extra McNugget! My father asked, "How many did we pay for?" I answered, "20." He asked, "How many did we get?" I answered, "21!" My father pulled over the car and asked, "What do you think we should do?" I, disregarding the life lesson my *father* was trying to teach me, emotionally answered as any ten-year-old would, "Let's keep it! They messed up, not us. Drive Dad before they come looking for us!"

My father told me we were going to go back, and I had to return the extra nugget He said if we bought 20 and they gave us 19, we were *due* an additional one. But if we only bought 20 and we were given 21, we are taking something for which we failed to pay. If we keep it knowing we neglected to pay, that is stealing. He told me, "Son, you have to take it back." I returned that McNugget and learned a lesson about the Golden Rule. If I had lost my wallet, car keys, cell phone, or any other item, I would want the person who found it, to return it to me. That's an example of "treat other people, the way you want to be treated."

When it comes to communication, the Golden Rule has a flaw. Can we always treat others exactly the way we want to be treated? I am an energetic and emotional person. I like to high five, knuckle pound, and give hugs that let you know I care. However, can I treat everyone that way? One of my best friends is a no-nonsense, task focused, blunt person. Can we be blunt and no-nonsense with everyone? My accountant is an analytical person who has her family's daily to-do list synced to their family phones, so everyone knows where everyone is supposed to be 24/7. Can she be that analytical with everyone? Treating other people the way you want to be treated works well in certain dynamics. There are times to treat people, not as you want to be treated, but instead, treat people the way they want to be treated. We should treat everyone with respect. We should strive to be kind to all.

History

Early in my career, I was trying to explain to my clients the history of behavioral science. Between the different variations and gathering historical perspectives, I realized I was not helping people, and worse, I was confusing them! I was a communication coach, who failed to communicate the history of communication! Each method has their advantages. Each may be hard to ascertain unless you have the fortitude to do what I did and read books, articles, videos, and journals on all styles. Here is a brief overview of behavioral science.

- ➢ 444. B.C. - This is the earliest known study of documented behavioral science. It originated with a Greek Philosopher named Empedocles. He felt that four external elements of the planet (Fire, Earth, Air, and Water), impacted our behavior.

- ➢ 400 B.C. - A Greek philosopher Hippocrates believed that four internal fluids dictated our emotions (Choleric, Sanguine, Phlegmatic, and Melancholic).

- ➢ 1921 – Carl Jung, a Swiss psychiatrist and psychotherapist who founded analytical psychology, and Isabel Briggs-Myers felt neither internal or external elements influenced our behaviors, but they were influenced more based on four thought processes (Thinking, Sensing, Feeling, and Intuition).

- ➢ 1928 - An American Harvard psychologist, named Dr. William Moulton Marston, published a book entitled, "The Emotions of Normal People." He stated that four personality styles are determined less by our thought processes but more by our actions and motivations (Dominant, Influence, Steadiness, and Compliance).

See if this makes any sense to you! According to DiSC, I am a high "i" as a People-Extrovert with my secondary style of Compliance just above my median point, and my Steadiness trait dropping below my midline. Does this mean anything to you?

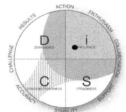

Leadership

If told this was the style of a new co-worker, how would you adapt?

Let's try the verbiage of another style. Let's look at Myers-Briggs (Isabell's and Jung's version). According to Myers-Briggs, I am an ENFJ, with Emotional being primary followed by an Intuitive nature combined with Feeling and Judgmental tendencies of behavior. Is this getting any better?

ISTJ	ISFJ	INFJ	INTJ
ISTP	ISFP	INFP	INTP
ESTP	ESFP	ENFP	ENTP
ESTJ	ESFJ	ENFJ	ENTJ

Empedocles 444. B.C.	Water	Air	Earth	Fire
Hippocrates 440 B.C.	Phlegmatic	Sanguine	Melancholic	Choleric
DiSC, 1928	Steady	Influence	Compliance	Dominance
Myers-Briggs, 1943	Intuition	Feeling	Thinking	Sensing
L.E.A.D. 2010	Laid Back	Energetic	Analytical	Direct

I created something I thought was simpler. I focused on three areas I felt were most needed by today's professionals.

1.   Understand the best communication styles.

27

2. Know their strengths and weaknesses.

3. Adapt based on each style's "do's" and "don'ts."

The approach is called L.E.A.D., as in leadership. Each letter represents the style. I created L.E.A.D. to help others simply and quickly identify and adapt to the different personalities relating to communication and leadership styles. L.E.A.D. can be applied from multiple perspectives

Question any assessment that tells you that based on your personality, you will be successful in a particular career. Here are three attributes that L.E.A.D. does not determine:

1. Ethics

2. Experiences

3. Skills

At age 19, I was a sophomore at Middle Tennessee State University. My college advisor told me to take an assessment that would align my answers to my ideal profession. I was then asked to complete the questionnaire. I answered, "Yes" to the following types of questions:

- Are you comfortable in front of large groups?

- Is leading others something you enjoy?

- Do you feel capable of driving your own success?

My results came back that I should be a Bus Driver!

L.E.A.D does not tell you what you should do with your life. In my opinion, no test or assessment can show you how to find joy in your life

L.E.A.D. Does Not Determine Your Ethics

Here is an example; if we take two people in history. Adolf

Hitler and Dr. Martin Luther King Jr., you would agree both men were comfortable in front of large audiences. You may also agree both men were persuasive. You may also agree both men were willing to die for what they believed was right. We could continue with other examples that can make them seem like they would get along. However, if we put both those men into a conference room and asked them to agree about the importance of human life, how do think that conversation would go? Although they may have communication similarities in their behavioral styles, their ethics make them different people.

L.E.A.D. Does Not Determine Skills and Your Experiences.

If you have siblings, you know you can live in the same environment around the same people but have different experiences. I have an older brother. We grew up in the same house and were raised by the same people, but we have different lives and different personalities.

When you look at these styles, your decision making, your experiences, all these elements make up the pieces of who you are. That is why I am quick to tell people you just can't learn a person's style and go "Ok, I know everything about them." You cannot put people in a box and assume you know their history.

Introvert vs. Extrovert

Let's look at two different terms: Introvert and Extrovert. If you are an introvert, this means you are comfortable thinking about what you want to say before you say it. If you are an introvert, you are comfortable if you are not the center of attention. If you are an introvert, you need more information before making big decisions. If you are an introvert, you need time to process things before you do it. If you are an introvert, it might make you uncomfortable moving too fast or making decisions if without gathering enough information. If you are a true introvert, the more important the decision, the more information you need. The more important the decision, the longer you need to wait.

Let's look at the extroverts. Extroverts are comfortable speaking their mind; they do not need all the facts to form an opinion. An extrovert is comfortable thinking quickly and speaking quickly. For a true extrovert, when they say something out loud, that is the first time they hear it too! For the true extrovert, the more important the decision, the faster they prefer to move.

What happens if the introvert needs information from the extrovert? If the introvert sends the extrovert an email and the introvert says, "I need to know the status of our project." How much detail is the introvert expecting? A lot! The extrovert gets that email, and they reply in one minute, with three bullet points. When that extrovert pressed that send button, what is on the extrovert's mind? I'm finished.

The introvert sees their reply. The introvert only sees three bullet points. They see all that white space in the email. What does the introvert do? "Excuse me, I need more detail."

Let's switch it. Let's say the extrovert now needs information. The extrovert picks up the phone. "Hey, I need the status of where we are, thanks." How much detail is the extrovert expecting? Not much at all. How long is the extrovert willing to wait for it? Not long. However, the introvert says "What, you need detail? Yes!" They begin gathering links, charts, spreadsheets, downloads, graphs, names. How is the introvert feeling about themselves when they send that email? Employee of the week baby! The email status from the Introvert may take a couple of days. Then the Extrovert, two days later, gets the Introvert's email. The Extrovert has probably forgotten about it by now. The Extrovert opens the email and sees spreadsheets, attachments, links, and charts.

Can you see the challenges between these two styles?

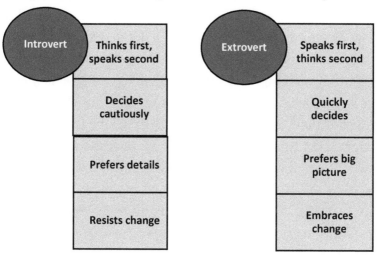

Task vs. People

There is another dichotomy. Consider communication and leadership styles of those who are people-focused versus task-focused. Task styles focus on completion. What is more important to a task person, feelings or facts? Facts. What is more important to a task person, relationships or results? Results. People styles want to know about your weekend. People styles want to know about your kids. People styles want to know if your grandmother's hip surgery went well.

Let's look at two managers. Let's say both were given a horrible task. Both must cut company expenses by $50,000. Both managers are told to eliminate a managerial position. The people manager must let somebody go. They must meet with someone Monday morning and terminate their position. Sunday night, how does the people manager sleep? Not well. What is on their mind? During the drive to work, what are they pondering? If the meeting starts at 9:00 am, how long might that meeting last with them? Maybe an hour, maybe taking them to lunch.

How would the Task person handle the same situation? The task person must let somebody go Monday morning. Sunday night, how are they are sleeping? Like a baby. What is on their mind as they are driving in? Getting their job done. Not just that one thing but everything they have on their to-do list. The meeting starts at 9:00 am, what are they doing at 9:19 am? Done. Let's say both styles meet later in the day in the parking lot. The people manager asks the task manager, "Hey task manager how's your day?" What does the task manager say? "Great, had ten things to do, I did twelve." How does the people manager feel about the task manager? Jerk, ice water in your veins. You let Harry go. They just bought that new house, what are they going to do? They just had a grandkid move in with them; I think their mom just turned ill. And you just let him go!

The task manager asks the people manager. "Hey, how was your day?" What does the people manager say? "Horrible, lousy day." Task managers are thinking, that was at 9:00 a.m., it's almost 6:00 pm, is that all you did today? What if these two styles must plan the holiday picnic?

Can you see some challenges between these two styles?

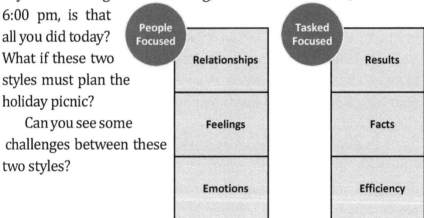

Leadership Styles

There are four styles of leadership. Each of the four styles, Laid Back, Energetic, Analytical, and Dominant, has their own approach. No one is right or wrong. I want you to learn how to adapt to them, how to talk to them, and the best way they can connect with you.

There is a term called a blend, and if you take my company's assessment, you receive a score from 0% to 100% measuring each of your style's. Only about 1% of the population are pure styles. According to personality testing from Inscape Publishing, some examples of Pure Styles are:

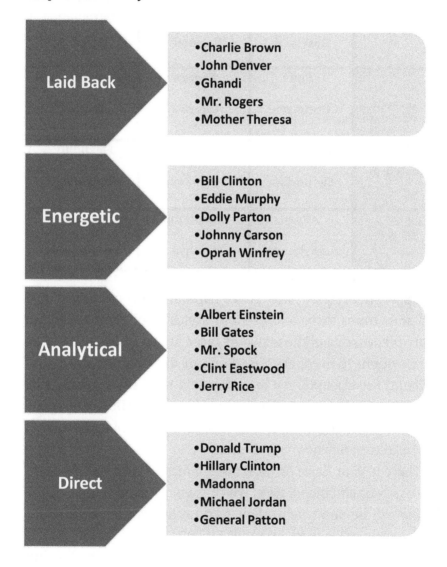

Laid Back
- Charlie Brown
- John Denver
- Ghandi
- Mr. Rogers
- Mother Theresa

Energetic
- Bill Clinton
- Eddie Murphy
- Dolly Parton
- Johnny Carson
- Oprah Winfrey

Analytical
- Albert Einstein
- Bill Gates
- Mr. Spock
- Clint Eastwood
- Jerry Rice

Direct
- Donald Trump
- Hillary Clinton
- Madonna
- Michael Jordan
- General Patton

Every L.E.A.D. Personality Has an Emotional Factoring Motivator, Called, Their E.G.O.

	Emotion	Goal	Obstacle
Laid Back	Hidden Reserved	Consistency Harmony	Confrontation Urgency
Energetic	Fun Optimism	Engage Interact	Follow- through Details
Analytical	Resistance Skepticism	Accuracy Process	Flexibility Spontaneity
Direct	Anger Impatience	Completion Control	Empathy People skills

Approximately 80% of us are combinations of at least two .and sometimes three of these four styles. Even though most of us are blends, one of those two or three styles is still going to be more evident than others based on our disposition during that moment. For example, you may be a Laid Back style. If somebody threatens your kids or challenges your belief, your Dominance may increase. However, once the crisis is over, what is going to happen? You will return to who you truly are.

There is your basic or born style, which is your Natural Style. There is your situational style, which is your Adaptive Style. Some people can be one way in their Natural Styles then be another way on projects in their Adaptive Styles.

I know people who are strong in their natural styles, but their job responsibilities do not allow them to exert their natural tendencies. They exude their natural traits in other outlets such as home, recreational activities, or in their communities.

When there is synergy between your natural and adaptive styles, you tend to have more joy. When there is an imbalance between your natural and adaptive styles, you tend to have more stress.

One of my clients is a true Dominant Style. He is a career counselor for aspiring college graduates. His Dominance wants him to look that 22-year-old person in the face and say, *"If you'd cut your hair, pull up your pants, use proper grammar, cover up your eleven tattoos, and take those piercings out of your face, you could probably get a job; now straighten up and get out of my office."* However, his job responsibilities require him to, ask, *"In which career field do you think you can best contribute?"* Who he wants to be and who his job asks him to be, are different. He enjoys the benefits the job provides to his family, and he knows occasionally he can help a young person. Although he is stressed, he feels his stress is justified.

My Mother is a retired member of the United States Army. She is not a dominant person, but since she wanted to make sure my brother and I had advantages, she worked three jobs to put us through private school. She committed to two tours in the Middle East. Although she is patriotic, she does not believe in hurting people. She justified her conflict to provide for my brother and me. She told me she would suppress her fear to make the sacrifices for our education, but we had to use the knowledge to make our lives better.

The best way to understand all four communication leadership styles of **L.E.A.D**. is to review each one individually.

Laid Back & Low Key

Traits	Challenges	Goals
• Listener	• Confrontation	• Consistency
• Reserved	• Disorganization	• Harmony
• Supporter	• Urgency	• Stability

Let's look at the first of the four styles. Coming in at 40% is the Laid Back and Low Key style. You will not get anywhere with these Laid Back styles by arguing. Laid back styles are typically non-confrontational people. If you get confrontational, they will shut down, and they will find a way to stay away from you.

The misconception about Laid Back styles is they are always quiet. That is partially accurate; behavioral science tells us that Laid Back styles are only quiet in large groups or around people with whom they feel uncomfortable. In small groups where they feel comfortable, they can be talkative. A true Laid Back style might not have 40 new friends they met this year. A Laid Back style may have four friends, but they have had those friends for a long time. How hard is it to earn the trust of a Laid Back style? Very hard. However, once you are in their circle, they will always support you. If you break the trust of a Laid Back style, how many second chances might you get? Perhaps few, if any. If they are kind enough to let you back in, is it ever the way it was before? They may remain polite, but there is going to be a separation. Other styles may be more forgiving. Laid Back styles hold trust and loyalty to a high degree.

One of the strongest traits of a Laid Back Style is their consistency. Laid back styles welcome and support routines. They have their preferred methods that have, over time, brought them value and fulfillment. A Laid Back style may initially resist a new method or idea. Even if an approach has supportive data, even if the new idea saves time, even if the new concept can save or earn more money, the Laid Back style might need time to adjust. It is not that the Laid Back is resistant to that specific change; the Laid Back style is simply resistant to change.

My Father has an eating routine. Wednesday dinner is always spaghetti. I remember in high school; on a Tuesday evening, my father took me to an awards dinner for student-athletes; they served fettuccine. The next day, on Wednesday evening, we go to his favorite Italian restaurant. To break my father from his culinary routine, I asked, "Dad, do you want to eat spaghetti two nights in a row?" He answered, "Last night we didn't have spaghetti; we had fettuccine. Tonight, we are having spaghetti."

Three Keys to Succeed when Communicating with Laid Back Low Key Styles

> ➤ Show appreciation.
> ➤ Avoid confrontation.
> ➤ Ask questions.

Laid Back & Low Key

Do	Do Not
Emphasize team	Get Loud
Provide deliberation time	Expect fast
Allow time for questions	Demand
Give steps	Leave them solo
Suggest follow-up times	Follow up only when due
Build trust	Assume
Reassure	Sell without validating
Establish rapport	Exclude their input

Energetic & Emotional

Traits	Challenges	Goals
• Talkative • Sociable • Gregarious	• Details • Follow up • Organization	• Be liked • Engage • Have fun

Let's look at the first extroverted style, the Energetic Emotional. The Energetic style is similar to the Laid Back style. Both the Laid Back style and the Energetic style are focused on people. The Laid Back and Energetic enjoy working with teams. How is the Energetic style different than the Laid Back style? The Energetic style is more extroverted and talkative. Another difference is, the Energetic style is more comfortable winging it in certain situations. Even if there is a process, even if there is a plan, the Energetic style is comfortable if the plan changes. The Energetic style may say, "Hey, let's just go with the flow and see what happens." How does a Laid Back style feel about winging it or going with the flow? Laid back styles want a path and a plan to follow. An Energetic style may look at the process and say, "Path? Let's make our own path." To adapt to the Energetic style, bring your personality, if you do not have one, borrow one.

Follow up with details in writing. That might mean by email, or it might mean by sticky note. Here is a typical conversation with an Energetic style. "Hey, that sounds great, let's get started on that next week, we'll get moving on it quickly, great, thanks see you soon!" What happens? They forget! To ensure your message registers with the Energetic Style; go back, leave them a voicemail, leave them an email, send them a text. Here is an example, of the type of message to leave when following up after a discussion with an Energetic style, "Great to know you agree with us about starting at 8:00 am on Monday. I will send you a follow-up reminder Sunday evening. I look forward to us finishing this by the 15th of June."

Energetic styles have the best of intentions, but they have a weakness in follow through. Energetic styles do not mean to disappoint anyone. They want to make everyone happy, but they sometimes overpromise. They are people pleasers. They do not mean to drop the ball; it is just that their strong drive to remain accommodating can supersede their focus of completion.

If an Energetic style walks into a room and nobody says anything to them, they may feel ignored. Energetic styles are comfortable being the center of attention. Since Energetic styles prefer interaction, they may focus more on their appearance. The Energetic style is most effective when engaged with others in a group environment.

Three Keys to Succeed when Communicating with Energetic and Emotional Styles

> ➤ Be optimistic.
> ➤ Have a follow-up plan.
> ➤ Make it engaging.

Energetic & Emotional

Do	Do Not
Bring personality	Be drab
Vary voice	Speak monotone
Use names	Be formal
Give overviews	Over analyze
Listen	Be all facts
Follow Up	Overtalk
Take notes	Wait
Socialize	Assume

Analytical & Accurate

Traits	Challenges	Goals
•Detailed •Logical •Pessimistic	•Ambiguity •Flexibility •Spontaneity	•Accuracy •Facts •Thoroughness

The Analytical and Accurate is our first "Task Style," at 14%, it is the smallest. This style might be the most misunderstood. This style is not trying to maintain consistency like the Laid Back style or make you happy like the Energetic style. The Analytical style focuses on accuracy. These are detailed-driven and quantifiable people. There is no such thing as kind of accurate, to these styles, there is just accurate. There is no such thing as bending the rules. If the meeting starts at 9:00 a.m., and you show up at 9:06 a.m., in their mind you are not a little late, you are late. If the cost is $99.14 is it about $100? To the analytical style, the cost is exact, $99.14. Analytical styles live in a world of quantifiable information. They are specific people. Words that aggravate them include: "estimate," "wing it," and "we'll get around to it." If you cannot give them facts, then give them examples. Analytical styles work better with specifics than opinions.

A team of executives held a marketing meeting to boost their country club's dwindling membership. They deliberately excluded a member of the team. Let's call this team member, "Ann." The team considered Ann a pessimist. They felt if they invited Ann to the meeting; she would berate ideas, criticize suggestions, and only point out flaws. Therefore, the team held an idea-generating meeting without her. The purpose of the meeting was to find a way to inform surrounding communities about the club's new features and services. The team decided to have business-card-sized coupons printed. The coupons offered: free golf lessons, couple's massages, reduced rate student memberships, etc. The coupons would be placed inside of helium balloons. The balloons would be released into the wind. Once the balloons landed, those who found them would remove the coupons from inside. The team felt once guests visited the club, they would see the value and would instantly want to join. They coordinated a publicity day. They invited media and city officials. Hundreds were scheduled to attend.

The morning before the marketing plan could be implemented; Ann addressed each member of the executive team stating, "It is not now nor, has it ever been my intent to discourage your fun. I feel sometimes our club's good ideas are not thought through completely. Our club has such a strong reputation for being a positive part of this community; I want to maintain our tradition of excellence. Regarding the dozens of helium balloons currently being kept in our recreation center, I hope you do not plan on setting them free today. The room erupts in grumbling, "Here we go again!" and "I knew she would say something like this!" Ann turned to exit the conference room then stopped at the door. She said, "According to Weather.com, a tropical storm has caused high winds from the Southeast. The winds may blow the balloons into the trajectory of the natural wildlife reserve located 44 miles from our club. When these balloons lose altitude, they will fall into the neighboring forestry. The local wildlife may eat these balloons. A few deceased animals may be considered normal. However, if there are several recently deceased animals within a ten-mile radius, the CDC (Center for Disease Control) may investigate. If they examine these animals, and the balloons containing our club's coupons are found to be the cause of their deaths, our club could be subject to fines threatening our club's goodwill."

The team agreed to cancel the press conference and rescheduled for two weeks later. Ann said that the balloon idea still had merit. Since they already invested resources in the balloons and the cards were beautifully designed, Ann suggested donating the balloons at local community fairs, shopping malls, and fresh markets. Club staff received permission to hand out the balloons at these events personally. The community liked meeting the club staff and getting to ask questions without having to drive to the club or leave voice messages. Within one year, the club increased their membership by 38%. Ann was promoted to the club's Marketing Director.

Analytical styles have little concerned about making projects fun or doing them fast. Analytical styles focus on the facts and how those facts lead to making better decisions.

Three Keys to Succeed when Communicating with Analytical and Accurate Styles

➤ Give them details.
➤ Research first.
➤ Respect their resistance.

Analytical & Accurate

Do	Do Not
Be specific	Be vague
Research first	Make assumptions
Focus on facts	Use opinions
Provide in writing	Say "trust", "hope", "try"
Give due dates	Allow unlimited review
Allow time	Forget parameters
Organize content	Ramble
Respect space	Dodge questions
Save the charm	Exaggerate

Dominant & Direct

Traits	Challenges	Goals
• Bottom-liners • Blunt • Risk takers • Competitive	• People skills • Patience	• Accomplish • Control

Let's look at our last style, the Dominant and Direct style. This style is called Dominant because they can have dominating personas in the room, on projects, or on teams. They are called Direct because they can be blunt.

Do not expect long answers from these styles. If a Dominant style likes it, they will tell you. If a Dominant style dislikes it, they will still tell you. Of the four styles of L.E.A.D., the Dominant style, at only 18%, is the second smallest. This style is all about efficiency. When they wake up every morning, and their feet touch the floor, they put everybody into two categories. They do not care if you are black, white, male, or female, 18 or 85. You are either on their to-do list, or you are in their way. Consider those whom you know who have this style.

Dominant people can say something others may feel is rude or blunt. The Dominant style is not considering feelings or how the comments can have emotional repercussions. They are trying to get things finished. In their minds, either you are helping them get things finished or you are keeping them from getting things finished.

They do not wake up thinking "I'm going to dislike you." They wake up saying "Here's what I have to do." Dominant styles are not trying to be popular. The Dominant style wants results! What if those results hurt people's feelings? What if those results might make some people upset? What if those results mean you might have to start over? What if those results mean you must spend more money? Where is their focus? It is on results.

The Dominant and Direct styles can be uncompromising when it comes to accepting excuses that others call reasons. Since the Dominant Style does not give many excuses, they rarely accept them. This does not mean this style is flawless. In fact, the Dominant style might make more mistakes due to their comfort with taking risks. When the Dominant style makes a mistake, they focus less time on the flaw and more time on what it takes to accomplish the result. Therefore, the Dominant and Direct style has high expectations of accountability from others, and they demand even more from themselves.

Dominant styles might not connect well with people. Dominant styles are less concerned with emotions, and more concerned with completions. The misconception is Dominant styles dislike people and have poor people skills. That is not true. The truth is, if you are a Dominant style, you dislike people who waste time. If you are a Dominant style, you dislike people who cannot get things finished. If you are a Dominant style, you dislike people who say they will and then they do not. If you are a sociable, friendly, chit-chatty person that gets things done, they may be fine with you. Be quick. If a dominant style asks you a "yes" or "no" question; answer with either, "yes" or "no." If you have more detail, which often the Analytical or Laid Back styles might have, answer their question first, then give them more detail. If a Dominant style asks, "*Is this finished?*," avoid answering like this, "*There are a few things we must consider, first...*" Answer them like this instead, "Not yet. We will finish it by Tuesday's deadline."

Three Keys to Succeed when Communicating with Dominant and Direct Styles

➢ Focus on finished.
➢ Save the details.
➢ Be quick.

Dominant & Direct

Do	Do Not
Be blunt	Be emotional
Be clear	Overuse opinions
Offer solutions	Over analyze
Speak briefly	Dodge accountability
Stay focused	Guesstimate
Meet deadlines	Take it personally
Be logical	Back down
Abbreviate facts	Lead with emotions
Answer directly	Give excessive details
	Be Vague

Consider this example of how the L.E.A.D. styles focus on different elements. A parent attended a little league soccer game. Their team lost in the championship game, 1 – 0. Here is how each style may reply when asked, *"How was the game?"*

Laid Back	It was a good season. Both teams showed great sportsmanship. To make it this far is quite an accomplishment.
Energetic	Wow! We almost had them! Ok, it was the final shot of the game. That number 10 from the other team, I think their name was Williams or Williamson, or, well anyway… this kid was practically unstoppable all year! They nailed the other team's only goal. Let me tell you, that kick was nothing short of a miracle shot. But you know what, now that our kids have had a taste of the performing on the big stage, we are going to be a force to reckon with next year!
Analytical	The only points scored was one penalty kick. That was the 4th point scored against our team in the last 13 months. The final score was Warriors 1 – Mountaineers 0.
Dominant	We lost.

The Laid Back style never mentioned the score, or victory, or defeat. The Laid Back style focused less on the game's outcome and more about how the team performed. To the Laid Back style, winning or losing came secondary to the teams' overall success.

The Energetic style felt compelled to give commentary highlights in the form a reconstructive story. They get sidetracked about the details but wants the listener to relive their emotion. The defeat is only briefly acknowledged, and immediately the Energetic style redirects their focus to the optimism of a next season.

Lead Out Loud!

The Analytical style gave only the facts. They replaced opinions with data. They gave statistics rather than commenting on perceptions of game effort. They Analytical even refers to the teams by their mascot names to be factual when sharing the score.

The Dominant style gave the game's final result. Notice how the Dominant style does not mention a score. Although if questioned, the Dominant style could provide more information, in their mind, they have fully answered the question.

Let's look at a professional example. During a team meeting, everyone is asked to give an idea of how to make the company better.

Laid Back	Let's have a "Thank you" Day. We can ask our customers to write us thank you letters about how we have helped them.
Energetic	We can have a cultural day food party! Let's have everyone bring in his or her best ethnic dishes to the office.
Analytical	How about distributing a regional wide survey to access the accuracy of last quarter's customer service rating scores?
Dominant	Give bonuses for results.

Identify which L.E.A.D. style is most likely to do the following:

Standing in a long line:

1___ Steps out of line and leaves.

2___ Calculates remaining time based on how many are in front.

3___ Starts a conversation with the person behind

or in front of them.

4___ Remains in line without engaging or will check their phone.

1. D; 2. A; 3. E; 4. L

Has the following voicemail message:

1___ Today is Thursday, August 4th. This is the answering service of Alexander Jay Williams. Please leave your name, your phone number, and a detailed message regarding the nature of your call. If this is an emergency, email your inquiry to info@helpdesk.com

2___ This is John, leave a message.

3___ Hello, I am sorry I missed your call. Please leave me a message. I will contact you as soon as I am able. Thank you very much.

4___ Hi, this is Frankie. I am either with a client or trying to find a new one. You could be the next one! Leave me a message, and I will personally call you back. My message to you is the same message my little league soccer coach said to me, "Soccer is just like life. Just keep smiling and keep kicking." Have a great day!

1. A; 2. D; 3. L; 4. E

Lead Out Loud!

Keys to Succeed

How soon are our L.E.A.D. personality styles noticeable in our behavior?

> I remember picking up my daughter, Taylor, from her elementary school. There were kids coloring on the floor. My daughter asked could she stay a bit longer. I agreed and took that as an opportunity to conduct some observational research (Yes, I am always working!). I wanted to see if I could recognize each child's communication characteristics regarding the four styles of L.E.A.D.
>
> There was Lauren. Lauren colored quietly in a small group of three other children. She hummed to herself while coloring. Although Lauren seemed friendly, she made no eye contact with the teacher, me, or the other kids. Lauren was having a Laid Back moment.
>
> There was a girl named Erica. Erica painted everything pink; the grass, the sky, and the water. Erica held up her picture and shouted, "Hey everybody, who wants to come with me to Planet Pinkville?" Erica was having an Energetic moment.
>
> There was Alex. Alex first traced the outline of everything he wanted to color. He then sharpened all his crayons. Alex laid them side by side like the bullets of an expert marksman at a shooting competition. Alex made sure to remain within the lines when coloring. Alex was having an Analytical moment.
>
> There was one boy named David. He wanted the green crayon but didn't have it. When he saw it in the hand of another child, David snatched the green crayon out of the hand of the other child. David was having a Dominant moment.

Learning L.E.A.D. gives you the advantage when negotiating, influencing, or communicating with others. Your personality strengths, whether they are: dominance, patience, charm, or intelligence; are limited unless you have the propensity to adapt to others.

> My first-grade teacher at O.L.P.H. (Our Lady of Perpetual Help) was Mrs. Howell. She would have all her students play a game that measured aptitude and cognitive thinking skills. There was a box that contained cut-out geometric shapes. Outside of the box were shapes of circles, squares, rectangles, and triangles. The goal was to see how fast you could place the right sized shapes inside of the box. If you could get all shapes inside of the box in under 60 seconds, you could play at recess. If it took you longer, you missed recess. I hated this game! It was not until I was 20 years old that I found out I was dyslexic. The shapes all seemed to be spinning and would never fit. I was the only kid in the class who could not figure out this game. I promised myself by next testing period, I would not only figure it out, but I would also solve this geometric box puzzle faster than anyone in the *class*.

> Next testing period, my goal was to place all geometric shapes in the box. All students passed with an average time of 50 seconds. The fastest was Jeff Howell who did it 39 seconds! I was the last child to go. I did it in 35 seconds! Mrs. Howell did not look excited about my results. She seemed disappointed. She said, "Now Vincent, you know that the square piece does not fit in the round hole." I looked down at all the shapes that were currently inside the box and said, "Mrs. Howell, if you push down hard enough, they all fit!"

Lead Out Loud!

The Laid Back styles want harmony. The Energetic styles want fun. The Dominant styles want efficiency. The Analytical styles want accuracy

Remember, the *key* is adapting!

CHAPTER CHALLENGE

Identify at least one "Do" and at least one "Do Not" that you will incorporate the next time you communicate with each style.

My Most Challenging Styles	How Will I Adapt?

Chapter 3:
The Spit Just Got Real -
Public Speaking

Lead Out Loud!

Would you rather give the eulogy or be in the casket? In surveys, most people rank fear of public speaking higher than death. It is true; most would rather be in the casket. However, how do we keep our careers from going (or staying) in the casket? The answer is to improve how you present yourself!

For many professionals, making effective presentations is the key to getting promotions, establishing authority, and increasing earnings, personally and for the company's bottom line. In many industries, speeches and presentations are sometimes necessary. It pays to become comfortable talking to groups.

Remember, it is normal to be nervous. The key to being a professional when you are nervous is to look and sound confident. When you look and sound confident, you are respected as competent. Become comfortable with being *un*comfortable!

Public speaking is more than talking in front of a crowd. Forget microphones, staring eyeballs, note cards and podiums. Consider these situations as opportunities of public speaking:

- Interviews
- Meetings
- Phone conferences
- Voicemails
- Toasts
- Acceptance of awards
- Video/Teleconferences
- Introductions
- Performance reviews
- Negotiations
- Debates
- Testifying in court
- Friendly arguments

- Not-so-friendly arguments
- Executive training
- Academic teaching
- Mentoring
- Leading
- Presentations

This chapter will help you amplify your attitude, confidence, preparation, audience adaptation, understanding the nature of presentations, delivery, and your overall skill of speaking before a group.

You will learn techniques to help you with each step of public speaking, from preparation to the delivery of a stellar presentation. Whether you are facing a crowd of hundreds or fifteen of the most important people in your company, the following information will help you amplify every opportunity!

Fear of public speaking consistently ranks as one of the top five phobias. We talk all day to each other, to pets, to children, sometimes even to ourselves! Why are we afraid to speak to a group?

We are not afraid of speaking in public; we are afraid of speaking to the public. One of the biggest fears most of us worry about is being perceived as foolish or inept. Then we let that worry grow until we are so anxious that it is hard even to breathe. Remember, it is normal to be nervous! Even in a small group situation or during an important conversation like a job interview, it is normal to feel anxiety. The key is not to let anxiety rule. Two ways to combat those feelings of fear are with **preparation** and **visualization**.

Preparation

Properly preparing for a presentation requires a fine balance. You need to know enough to demonstrate your expertise, but you do

Lead Out Loud!

not want to go overboard when imparting what you know. Have you ever felt trapped at a party listening to someone describing their hobby? Following these steps will ensure your audience does not feel trapped.

Narrow Your Topic

Being an expert on all aspects of business would be impossible. Even sales or customer service would be huge topics to cover in a presentation. Whittling your topic down is an important component to presenting like an expert.

Leaving a voice mail is an effective way to practice narrowing your topic. When you leave a message, be concise, giving only critical information. If you want someone to call you back but get distracted talking about a meeting scheduled for the following week, you have left an ineffective voice mail. To help yourself define your speech, call yourself and leave a voicemail about what you will cover. Practice talking out your idea. Then listen to that voicemail and evaluate your topic's depth and breadth.

List Your Main Points

Creating a list of the main points will serve as a working outline as you prepare. The more you learn, the easier it is to get sidetracked. Returning to your original list will help you stay focused on your narrowed topic.

Comfort is another advantage of keeping a list of main points throughout the preparation process. The more comfortable you are with that list, the more comfortable you will be talking about it. When you know your content, you speak with increased comfort!

Gather Facts

Collect data and customize your presentation to make it relevant to your audience. Examples that made sense ten years ago could be confusing today. Imagine a technology speech where the presenter talks about cassette tapes as "cutting-edge."

Fact gathering is where the temptation to over-prepare comes in. Including too many facts takes your talk into the realm of boredom — where no speaker (or listener) wants to be! Refer to your main points and keep the narrow scope of your topic in mind.

Question Yourself

As you research, keep a running list of questions that cross your mind. Chances are your audience will have those same questions. Keeping a list will help you remember to answer those questions for them.

Answering audience questions, even unasked ones, is a way of keeping them engaged. Anticipating questions and addressing them also builds your authority. I love the opportunity to ask questions in Q & A sessions, but I also like it when speakers ask and answer their own questions. When you question yourself, you can plan to ask and answer questions in your speech. Think about when you hired an expert, like an electrician or child care provider. Did you feel more at ease when they asked and then answered questions you were pondering? Inform your audience that at the end of your presentation you will invite questions from the group. When your audience anticipates interaction with you, they pay attention!

Once you have done the research and have a clear idea what you want to say, begin focusing on *how* you want to say it. Avoid the following:

- Reading your speech

- Memorizing your speech

- Being robotic

Unfortunately, most of us have sat through a presentation where the speaker seemed so uncomfortable, or bored, he or she resembled a machine. When you memorize every word, you run the risk of sounding lifeless and uninterested. When you read every word, eye contact is minimal; this makes it harder to engage your audience. When you learn to deliver your speech without memorizing or reading, this enables you to look and sound natural and spontaneous.

Create Cues

You **do** want to figure out exactly how to begin and end your presentation. Knowing your opening statement will help keep you from "umming" and "uhhing" at the beginning. Knowing your closing lets you know when to stop talking. As long as you keep those scripted sentences down to one or two at the very beginning and end, you will not sound automated. Practice the opening and closing enough that they become natural; meaning you can deliver them flawlessly.

Another way to help remember what you want to say is using physical cues. Connecting the main point with a move to the right or the left can help you know where you are in the progression of your presentation.

One reason it is tempting to write your speech or use note cards is, most people are afraid they will forget their main points and want the cards as a map through the speech. Using cues gives you the same kind of map but allows you to remain engaged with the audience.

Practice, Practice, Practice

Practice is the key to becoming comfortable with what you will say. The thing you should not expect is to be able to just "go over it in your head" a few times or to need only one practice. Schedule several practices into your preparation time, and you should start practicing your presentation as soon as you have a topic and some facts.

Knowing you have chosen a narrow topic, conducted the necessary research, and practiced enough to feel good about how you look and sound, you can reduce worry. Proper preparation alleviates fear and boosts confidence. It does not always banish the public speaking phobia completely — some people still might prefer the coffin to the eulogy.

Develop & Maintain Public Speaking Confidence The Four M Technique©

The Four M Technique represents four phases or transitions of thought. The purpose is to mentally prepare yourself to perform at your best even if you feel at your worst. The Four "M's" in the Four M Technique stands for, *"Making My Mental Movie."* This is when you imagine yourself performing perfectly during a moment of challenge. The Four M Technique has origins rooted from other tools such as meditation and the incorporation of visualizations.

Regardless of the effectiveness of an approach, striving to prepare yourself to overcome fear due to lack of preparation is futile. Avoid placing that level of stress on yourself. Instead, focus on these two aspects.

Focus on the ideal outcomes. Focus less on failing and more on succeeding. For example, if you are applying for a job, do not focus on what you will do if they ask you a question for which you are inadequately prepared. Instead, imagine yourself answering questions with confidence. Here is another example; if you are going to give a speech; instead of being afraid of looking or sounding incompetent, imagine yourself speaking with confidence and clarity.

Apply all five senses: sight, smell, taste, touch, and sound. Below are examples of incorporating all senses when using the Four M Technique.

Examples of The Four M Technique©

Sense	Speech Presentation	Conversation Negotiation
	Eye contact Conference room Smiles	Positive facial expressions Notepads Office setting
	Coffee/Beverages Markers	Paper/ink Tea Lotion
	Agreement Your strong voice Clapping	Controlled tone Chair squeaking Them saying "yes."
	Fresh mints Cool water	Fresh mints Cool water
	Feet firm Strong handshakes Body temperature	Note taking material Sitting or standing Typing ideas

The following content does not vary based on gender, age, race, sexual orientation, or heritage. Our brains have two parts or hemispheres. There is a line of nerves banded together called the corpus callosum. These banded string of nerves separates the left and right sides of our brains.

The left side of our brains controls vocabulary and logical thinking. The right side of our controls emotions and involuntary muscular movements (breathing, eye blinks, etc.).

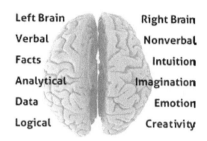

To get started, follow these four steps:

1) Seclude.

2) Close.

3) Imagine.

4) Incorporate.

Step 1: Seclude - Find a quiet place to be alone.

You will want some privacy, especially if you are just beginning to use this technique. Sitting at your desk or standing in a crowded elevator may not be ideal for practicing step one.

Find a place where you will not be interrupted and where you can control the level of noise. Some convenient places I recommend are a silent room, an isolated location in your office building, in your car or even the bathroom (get a stall if one is available).

Step 2: Close – Shut out noise.

Simply closing off external distractions can reduce tension by as much as 30%. Close your eyes. Turn off televisions, radios, or anything that makes noise. Make your environment as quiet as possible.

Step 3: Imagine – See yourself at your best.

Be specific in your mind. Create an ideal place of peace. It can be a location you visited several times or only once, or it could be somewhere you have never visited but only read or heard about. To your brain, it does not matter. What matters is you feel euphoric and at peace.

Step 4: Incorporate.

Think about how that place smells, the temperature, the texture of your clothing, what it sounds like, what you might be eating or drinking and what you might see. Use these details to immerse yourself in that experience. Creating a mental movie causes the right hemisphere of your brain (the creative part that is gullible and easy to fool) to do all the things it would do if you were really in that happy place. That portion of your brain sends signals for your muscles to relax. This process increases the release of the hormone dopamine which is a neurotransmitter that helps regulate and control your brain's pleasure mechanism.

Fear and courage are both decisions.
Courage is admitting fear and still doing what it takes.

Use this four-step approach to develop and maintain confidence when speaking in public it only takes a little practice to learn how to "trick" your brain into relaxing. You may even find this technique can help you in other stressful situations.

While you may always feel some nervousness before a presentation, this tool reduces that stress and makes stepping on stage or up to the podium easier. To do any job well, you need the right tools. A carpenter must have a hammer, and a surgeon needs a scalpel. Public speakers need visualizations.

To understand how visualization works, think about your last dream. If it was unpleasant, you might have awoken tired, stressed, and full of tension. If you had an especially pleasant dream, you might have awoken happy, relaxed, and maybe energized. You can create that feeling anytime you want by creating a "mental movie."

A mind movie is more than simply thinking about a relaxing place or successful moment. It is reliving or creating the entire experience, including as many details as possible. The key is incorporating all your senses (smell, sight, sound, touch, and taste) so your brain believes it is happening.

Instead of imagining yourself on a beach or your ideal dream location, incorporate the place where you will speak. Imagine yourself delivering the perfect speech. Picture the entire presentation, with as many details as you can conjure. Include the faces of the audience, the feel of the lights, the smell of the markers, the sounds of the crowd, or anything else you can incorporate.

Make this visualization positive. Think of yourself confidently walking to the microphone and the audience positively responding. A detailed visualization of a perfect delivery is not a guarantee it will happen that way, but it is an effective way to build and maintain your confidence. In the same way professional basketball players visualize the ball going through the hoop when they take free throw shots, visualize yourself giving a successful communication encounter. It is wise to practice making mental movies well before your presentation. Don't worry! You will enjoy the practice!

To be at your most effective at public speaking, you must first believe in yourself and your message.

Lead Out Loud!

A former client contacted me about helping one of his managers named Harry. The client told me Harry was up for a promotion. Harry did not like change or speaking in public. If promoted, Harry would be required to give a five-minute presentation at a different regional office every month.

Harry was terrified of speaking in public. He understood the promotion was good for him and his family, and he accepted the advancement. Initially, Harry was reluctant when told he had to improve his public speaking skills. He said he worked for the company for eleven years without having to give a speech or travel to new locations.

Harry was so nervous during our first few sessions that he forgot his name. It had taken almost a week before he was comfortable seeing and hearing his recordings. After a few coaching sessions with me, Harry still had reservations about being in front of audiences. However, his manager and audiences told him, "Wow! You can explain things in such a clear manner; it is like you were born to do this job!"

Harry admits he would still rather sit down and discuss the job over a cup of coffee than being the center of attention. However, he learned to embrace the opportunity to help new members.

Harry thanked me for not giving up on him despite his strong fear. Harry is no longer with us, and his company named an award "The Harry Heart Award." It is given to only one employee every year and reads: "Have a Heart Like Harry. Conquer Your Fears to Be an Example of Courage for Others."

When I met Harry, he asked me, "You mean to tell me

your job is to travel all over the place? Traveling from company to company? Talking in front of a room full of strangers?" I told him, "Yes, sir." He put his hand on my shoulder and said, "Don't get too *discouraged* young feller. Hang in there. Something good and steady will come along one of these days."

**Being nervous is what makes you human.
Being prepared makes you professional.**

Purpose

Public Speaking is as Easy as P.I.E.

You need to understand the goal of your speech and understand who will make up your audience. Those two pieces of information give you a goal and a target — they tell you how to customize your presentation. When you know the reason for your talk, you can convey your ideas with increased clarity. When you know something about the people who will be hearing it, you can speak at the appropriate level. In every speech, you are doing one of the following three things: Persuading, Informing, or Engaging.

Some presentations combine two or even all three purposes, but usually, one element is most important:

- If you are presenting at an industry conference, you may want to primarily **inform** your audience of something, but you may also want to **persuade** them to take advantage of learning more through a course you sell or a service you offer.

- During a job interview, your primary goal is to **persuade** the manager to hire you, but you also need to **inform** him or her about your background.

- A toast or an acceptance speech should be **engaging** but can also contain an element of **persuasion** if you want others to take action.

> **Don't let your audience change your message.**
> **Let your message change your audience.**

Persuade

Get Your Audience to Take Action or Encourage Thought.

Presentations designed to persuade surround us daily. Every television commercial, billboard, political speech, and sales pitch is supposed to persuade us to take action. Likewise, sales professionals, managers, and entrepreneurs must make persuasive presentations to succeed.

When called upon to persuade, you must convince your audience to either do something or think a certain way. You may want them to purchase something, visit a website, call a number, or learn more about a topic. To persuade them, use verbs and give specific examples. Show the benefits of that action and the consequences of not taking it.

Using a comparison, either with images or descriptions is a classic type of persuasion. Bounty Paper Towel commercials pair a catchy slogan, "the quicker picker-upper," with images of a comparison product. Many commercials for products use the same tactic because it is powerful, and it works.

Using stories in persuasive speeches allows your audience to imagine the real-world benefits of your product, service, opinion, or position. When you can build empathy with the people listening, you gain their trust. How much more likely are *you* to purchase from someone you trust versus someone who seems unethical? Using anecdotes and personal stories allows you to be sincere in your speaking.

Inform

Present Unbiased and Non-Opinionated Information

Some presentations are simply to deliver information. In certain business situations, it is imperative to avoid trying to persuade the audience and instead simply share information. People often attend conferences, lectures, and association meetings to consume information.

Statistics, facts, and data often show up in informational presentations. Avoid offering an opinion about the numbers and factual content. Focus only on informing audience members. Usually, the tone of an informative presentation is more serious than a persuasive or engaging one.

An example of a speech that informs would be presenting quarterly results to a board of directors. In such a situation, you would simply be sharing numbers and statistics. Charts and diagrams make useful visual aids for informative presentations.

The fact that you are not trying to persuade your audience to a particular point of view does not mean that your presentation must be as dry as three-day-old pound cake. If you want the audience to remember the information, you need to take steps to make your presentation memorable. This is where many informative presentations hit a stumbling block.

Using a mnemonic device, using appropriate humor including a story, or displaying complementary images, can help your audience retain information. You want to give your facts a setting, so audience members have a context for remembering them.

In the introduction, I provided a setting for the fact that people rate their fear of public speaking higher than their fear of death by using the casket/eulogy illustration. Picturing yourself either at a podium giving a eulogy or lying in a casket is much more likely to stick in your memory than simply reading the sentence "People are more afraid of public speaking than of death."

Lead Out Loud!

Engage

Establish an Emotional Connection with Storytelling

Think of your favorite comedians, teachers, or other interesting people. Chances are, they all are good storytellers.

Of course, you always want to engage your audience. In some situations, just telling a story and connecting with your listeners is the primary purpose of your presentation. A keynote speech is not usually meant to persuade, nor is the purpose solely to deliver information. Instead, a keynote speech seeks to engage the audience's feelings.

Networking events are a less formal time to give engaging "speeches." You attend networking events to meet people and make contacts. It helps if those people remember you later! Amplify your engagement, and you will increase the likelihood of being remembered. Here are tips that will help you give an engaging presentation:

- Encourage interaction. Ask questions and welcome reactions.

- Be sincere. People sense fakery. Mean what you say.

- Speak specifically. Generalities are boring!

Let's look at the three purposes in closer detail. Even if your topic is food, you can speak on this topic to Persuade, Inform, or Engage.

Persuade: Eat two green vegetables for dinner for the next thirty days.
Inform: There are five types of leafy green vegetables.
Engage: How I lost fifteen pounds by eating more fruits and vegetables.

Structure Your Message

Presenting is stressful enough without having to memorize all your content. Remember, never memorize. Instead, you should learn! The best way to learn your presentations is to make the content easier to remember and deliver. Never write out a speech in its entirety. If you do, you will feel obligated to say it exactly the way you wrote it. There is a different rhythm to writing a speech than giving a speech. Even if the speech is well-written, it could fall flat when delivered. There are good reasons to write out portions of your speech for practice but writing the whole thing could throw you off during your actual presentation.

Instead, use an outline. When you go to a restaurant, you ask for a menu. It does not have excessive content or long explanations of the food. The menu offers quick, simple explanations to give you just enough insight to make a good selection. While a menu may say "Creamy Potato Soup," it does not list all the ingredients. However, you still can enjoy all the details that went into its preparation. The menu is an outline. It does not contain every word you say in a speech; it lists the main points to enable you to remain free to enjoy the natural rhythm of speaking without being anchored by memorization.

To create a speech outline, write just enough so that your brain will recall all the details you want to include. Do not worry about remembering all the facts. With proper practice, the facts will flow. In the speech outline, focus on remembering key points. The outline should have the following content:

> ➢ Purpose

> ➢ Opening

> ➢ Main Point

> ➢ Supportive Data

> ➢ Conclusion

Speech Outline Key Content

Purpose	Determine if you want to persuade, inform, or engage.
Opening	Begin with a question, quote, story, or a statistic.
Main Point	State your intentions of giving the presentation.
Supportive Data	Add content that validates your purpose.
Conclusion	End with a question, quote, story, or a statistic.

Here are three examples of speech outlines.

1. Purpose: **Persuade** Inform Engage

Topic	Open at least two bank accounts.
Opening Statement	A story about the benefits of having a checking and savings account.
Main Point 1	Establish a relationship with at least two banks.
Quote	Dave Ramsey, the author of New York Times best-seller, "The Total Money Makeover," says, *"You've got to tell your money what to do, or it will leave you."*
Question	What would you do if told to invest $10,000?
Statistic	According to Statistic Brain, an online resource for financial consumers, only 21% of Americans say they balance their checkbooks.
Conclusion	Suggest how to get started.

2. Purpose: ___Persuade___ **Inform** ___Engage___

Topic	Carl Lewis and Jessie Owens
Opening Statement	Story about Lewis and Owens
Quote	Jessie Owens, four-time track & field gold medalist, said to Carl Lewis, *"You are a skinny kid, but you can beat the bigger kids if you work harder."*
Question	What identical accomplishment did both Carl Lewis and Jessie Owens achieve?
Supportive Data	Jessie Owens won four gold medals in the 1936 Olympics. Carl Lewis won four gold medals in the 1984 Olympics.
Conclusion	Give closing statement for more information.

3. Purpose: Persuade   Inform   **Engage**

Topic	Toast, as the best man or maid of honor
Opening Statement	Statistic: *According to Tango.com, a website dedicated to relationship longevity, 70% of happy couples have similar interests.*
Story	Share how you introduced the couple.
Question	What is it like marrying your best friend?
Supportive Data	Dr. Phil McGraw, author, and psychologist says, *"Never put more into a relationship than you can afford to lose."*
Conclusion	Let's raise our glasses to the happy couple!

Of course, you would not read your outline. In fact, you should not even carry it on stage or in front of your audience. The outline will help you practice. It will help you cement your main points.

Lead Out Loud!

Develop a Presentation Outline Review

Purpose	• Determine if you want to persuade, inform, or engage.
Opening	• Begin with a question, quote, story, or a statistic.
Main Point(s)	• State your intentions of giving the presentation.
Supportive Data	• Add content that validates your purpose.

Nonverbal Messages

Control Your Body Language

Which is more important, what you say or how you say it? Before you answer, consider approximately 93% of your audience's opinion of you is based on factors *other* than what you say. How you look is important and contributes to 55% of their opinion. How you sound makes a 38% difference in what they think of you. This means only 7% of the audience's opinion is based on your words! Words are important. How you look and how you sound is vital. Focus less on researching the perfect synonyms and spend more time getting your body language and voice to demonstrate your comfort, competence, and confidence.

One of the most uncomfortable aspects of speaking in front of a group, or even having a conversation with someone new, is figuring out how to stand, where to put your hands, where to look, or even how much to move. Body language is one of the aspects most of us sense in others, rather than control in ourselves. It is interesting, and a little scary, to realize that other people could know more about your body language than you do.

Analyzing what you do with your body when you are relaxed and comfortable with your surroundings is an important part of knowing what to do when you are speaking in front of a group, attending a networking event, or charming a hiring manager. Once you know what your natural body language preferences are, you can polish and refine your posture, your hand gestures, and your overall movements, to ensure your body conveys the appropriate messages.

Always speak within your comfort zone. Whether you are an upbeat or low-key person, you will give presentations the way you usually speak. Don't force the flow, just relax and let it go! For example, if you are a gregarious and energetic person when you are comfortable, it is unrealistic to practice being stationary behind a podium, reciting an avalanche of facts. On the other hand, if you are a low-key and reserved person, it is unrealistic to think you will turn into a boisterous, laugh-a-minute speaker. Be comfortable being the type of speaker you are naturally.

Initial impression- The opinions formed about you by your audience when they first see you.

As soon as your audience sees you, they begin judging you.

Lead Out Loud!

The good news is, if you convey confidence during their initial impression by having your head up, your back straight, moving with a smooth stride, and making eye contact, their positive initial impression of you will last. The bad news is if you give a weak initial impression: head down, low energy, and no eye contact, their initial negative impression of you will last.

The initial impression can start before your introduction. It can start when you enter the room, as soon as you step off the elevator when you walk in the building or even when you are pulling into the parking lot. As the speaker, you are ALWAYS on!

Initial Impression

Do the following to make a stronger entrance:

- Smile.
- Greet others.
- Establish eye contact.
- Put paprika in your pep and step.

Posture

At a party with your closest friends, how do you stand? While many of us need to work on posture in general, some people are just terribly slouchy when they are comfortable. There is a happy medium between stiff and "at attention" and slumping.

Take note of your posture when you are relaxed. Look at yourself standing at ease in the mirror. You may need to adjust, but the stance you see is your starting point.

Compare your posture to people you think of as confident. What is it about their posture that makes them seem confident? Are their arms to the side, stiff and unmoving? Are they slouching or standing military straight? What are their feet doing?

Establishing a stance that is comfortable and natural, but that also shows you are confident and relaxed, requires you to mix what you do and what you want to do. Simply making an effort to notice body language is the first essential step to exuding authority and confidence when speaking in front of a group.

How Should I Stand?

- Keep your head up to establish and maintain eye contact.
- Relax your shoulders, allowing gravity to pull them down.
- Keep your back straight, even when sitting.
- Align your feet to be shoulder-width apart.
- Place your feet flat on the floor.
- Point your toes toward your audience.
- Keep your feet still unless you are deliberately walking for emphasis.

Head Positioning

How you hold your head may seem like an insignificant detail, but, the tilt of your head and where your eyes are looking make an enormous difference in the message you send through body language. When we meet new people, we form unbelievably fast opinions about them. We may base those decisions on details as intricate as to how a person holds his or her head.

Think of cliché sayings like "chin up," or "hold your head high." People say those things for a reason, the position of your head tells the world something important. When your head is bowed, you appear beaten, tired, or overwhelmed. When you hold your head up, you appear determined, confident, and authoritative.

How Should I Position My Head?

- Align it with your body.
- Keep ears parallel to the walls.
- Avoid tilting unless complementary to the message.

Lead Out Loud!

Eye Contact

Look at your audience, NOT at the walls, floors, ceilings or note cards. If you look at the floor, then at the ceiling, then out of the window, your audience will perceive you as nervous. Your audience can perceive direct, unbroken, and intense eye contact as intimidating. As with establishing recommended posture, the appropriate amount of eye contact is a balance.

Plenty of imaginative suggestions have been traditionally passed around about where to focus your eyes to feel more comfortable while speaking. Have you heard:

- Gaze at a spot on the back wall of the room?
- Scan the top of people's heads?
- Imagine everyone in your audience without any clothes?

Have any of these ever helped you look or feel more comfortable?

Where Do I Look?

- Establish eye contact.
- Look at their faces. Connect with the eyes of attendees in distant rows if the audience is large.
- Avoid looking at floors, ceilings, walls, podiums, windows, or—dare I say it—note cards!

One of the many reasons you should not carry note cards on stage is you will look at them instead of at the audience. I would rather hear a B+ speech from the speaker without note cards than to have an A+ speech read to me.

There are exceptions. I was the emcee at an international event. Three minutes before the event started, announcing the winners and special guests were added to my hosting responsibilities. Some of the names were hard to pronounce: Mukapadia, Kjos, and Xiong. I phonetically wrote their names on note cards to ensure I said them correctly. After saying their names, I deliberately tore up the cards in front of the audience then proceeded to emcee without touching another notepad all evening.

Facial Expressions

Your facial expressions are an essential element of your body language. When you practice and learn to control your expressions, you gain a powerful tool. You can choose to use your facial expressions to completely negate the words coming out of your mouth if it serves your purpose. Alternatively, your facial expression can "speak" to excitement, even if your words are calm and quiet.

As you practice your delivery, try varying your facial expressions in unexpected places. You may find that a strategically placed expression can emphasize your point. Once you have practiced, experimented, and identified how you could best use facial expressions, keep practicing!

Facial expressions and gestures serve as physical cues just as stepping to the right or left. If you are presenting in a large venue, facial expressions may not be the most efficient way to emphasize your point, unless a camera is projecting you on a larger screen. Your overall body language is always important. In a bigger setting, remember to make your gestures bigger so they will be visible from far away.

What Should I Do with My Face?
- Look like you want to be there.
- Smile.
- Show facial expressions complementary to the message.

Hand Gestures

Often my clients and students asked me, "When I am speaking, what do I do with my hands?" At most conferences, social gatherings, or professional events, you can hold a notebook, a drink, or even a pen, so you are relieved of the worry about what to do with your hands. However, standing in front of a group, your hands can suddenly feel like lead weights attached to the ends of your arms.

If you normally avoid using many hand gestures during a conversation, you will feel unnatural if you try to use them during a presentation. The opposite is true as well; holding your hands still if you normally move them will feel strange.

What Do I Do with My Hands?

- Relax.
- Gesture between your waist and shoulders.
- Make movements deliberate and smooth as opposed to jerky and abrupt.
- Gesture outside of the range only when complementary to the message.

Walking

Fight or flight is the body's natural response to any perceived external threat. Under duress, you will either defend against the threat (fight) or run from it (flight). In speech, there is a similar response to consider regarding how your body will naturally want to react under the stress of giving a speech.

When giving a presentation, you should either "plant" or "pace." When you plant, it means you cement your feet to one spot and never move until you walk off stage. When you pace, it means you deliberately pick up your feet and walk during your speech.

If you pace, avoid crossing your feet, or you risk tripping. Only take three steps at a time. Avoid walking and talking simultaneously. Speak—stop talking — pace three steps — start talking.

Feet Positioning

Your head and heart may say, "Stay." Your feet may say, "Let's hurry up and get out of here!" Listen to your head and heart. Position your feet to look and feel stable. Even if you prepared well, practiced often, and feel confident, continually shifting your feet will make the audience think you are nervous.

If you are behind a podium, you can cheat and move your feet. If you shift too much, even behind a podium, it will affect your overall posture. If you are fortunate, you will speak without a podium — yes, speaking without a podium is a good thing!

How Should I Position My Feet?

- Place both feet flat.
- Keep both feet still.
- Place feet shoulder-width apart.
- Point toes toward your audience.

The more you move during your speech, the more excitable and upbeat you will appear. The less you move during your speech, the more serious and controlled you will appear.

EXCITEMENT

Hand gestures, Facial Expressions, and Movement

SERIOUS

Phipps Practice Tip

Practice improving your body language by videotaping yourself, then play back the recording with the sound turned off. Ignore what you said. Focus on *how you look* while saying it. Observe your posture; look at your hand gestures; watch your facial expressions, and examine all aspects of our body language.

Lead Out Loud!

Do you want to improve your body language? Show your video to a critical person you trust. Play it with the mute button on. Simply ask, "How confident do I look?" Whatever they say, thank them, take note, and see what you can do to improve.

Phipps Body Language Tip

Because almost 60% of the impression of you formed by your audience is based on your body language, make sure you focus on looking comfortable.

Control Your Voice

It is the stuff of nightmares: You step up to the podium, take a breath and make the initial statement you have practiced many times, but all that comes out is a squeak. Horrified, you take a gulp of water—spilling half of it down your shirt — and try again. This time, only a breathy whisper escapes. After an experience like that, you may wake up in a cold sweat, with heart pounding and fear forming a ball in your stomach. No wonder some people rate fear of public speaking higher than fear of death!

Following the tips in this chapter will help you avoid such a nightmare scenario and deliver your words confidently, in a strong and clear voice. Previously, we talked about practicing your presentation with a video camera with the sound muted. Now, it is time to turn up the volume — fearlessly.

Common voice problems are:

- **Volume** (too loud or too soft)
- **Pausing** (too short or too long)
- **Rate** (speaking too quickly or too slowly)

Some of those problems will fade away naturally when you feel confident about your presentation. When you know what you want to say, and you have practiced saying it, you feel less nervous. Preparation goes a long way toward establishing a strong voice.

Volume and Speed

EXCITEMENT

↑

Volume and Speed

↓

SERIOUS

Volume is important. If you are too quiet, people give up trying to figure out what you are saying. If you are too loud, people will spend more time wondering why you are yelling than paying attention to your message.

One of the best ways to stand *out* is to speak up.

If you will be using a microphone, the matter of volume is slightly more complicated. With a microphone, you must adjust your volume and find the best distance from your mouth to the microphone. If you are too far away, the microphone is useless. Too close and, well, we have all had the unhappy experience of listening to a speaker holding the microphone too close! If possible, practice with the microphone. Often, you do not have that opportunity. In that case, deliver your opening sentence to get comfortable. Closely observe anyone who speaks before you do and note how they sound and where they stand. Even though it may not seem like it, a microphone does make it easier to speak normally, and it does not take long to get used to using it.

A fire hose turned on high is powerful. Yet, if left unattended to writhe and spray at random, the water will spray around without extinguishing any flames. When channeled and controlled, that fire hose can stop the fire in a flaming building. Your volume is powerful. When controlled, it can douse a flaming situation or ignite a presentation.

Volume drops occur when you are speaking, and your sound inexplicably gets lower. You sound as if you are running out of air. If this happens, your audience will see you as losing confidence or being confused. You drop your volume because the left hemisphere (logical part of the brain that also controls vocabulary) tells you, "I am almost out of words. The right side of your brain, which controls breathing, says "I don't need that much more air. Prepare to shut down."

Volume swells or "Hards" are when you unnecessarily speak louder. Sometimes, only a keyword or phrase is said louder, and the volume does not fit with your message. Your audience will see you as sporadic and lacking control.

When you finish your sentences with strong volume, no swells, and no drops, you sound confident and competent. Get comfortable hearing how you sound. You will become comfortable speaking. When you are comfortable speaking, it is evident in your voice, and others enjoy and even anticipate listening to you.

Phipps' Practice Tip for Volume and Speed

Increase volume and speed to show excitement.
Decrease volume and speed to show seriousness.

The Power of the Pause

A pause is a powerful tool. You can add emphasis, increase tension, or simply give yourself a moment to think. However, you need to be careful with the length of your pauses.

Let's get specific. If you begin paying attention to pauses in normal conversation or speeches given by professionals, you will find that a typical pause lasts from one to three seconds. A short pause is one to two seconds. A long pause is two to three seconds. A pause over four seconds is too much.

Pause Scenarios

Pause Scenario #1

Question: How do I look?

Typical pause: 1-2 Seconds

Answer: You look great!

Pause Scenario #2

Question: How do I look?

Awkward pause: 4+ Seconds

Answer: You look great.

(See, it gets weird! With too much time to think, the response is questioned.)

- Pause before beginning your speech.
- Pause before and after saying a main point.
- Pause to allow audience interaction.
- Insert pauses at different points in your speech.
- Vary pause length to find the best use.

Well said beats well read.

Vocal Rhythm

Everyone has listened to a speaker who spoke endlessly in a dry, monotone "rhythm." It is boring beyond words to listen to someone who speaks with no vocal variation. Take note of how much your vocal range varies in a regular conversation.

Lead Out Loud!

Your voice gets higher toward the end of a question and trails off when you make an insinuation. Vocal rhythm provides interest, character, flavor, and texture to your words. Do not try to eliminate all swells and drops from your speech, and do not make it your goal to speak at the same rate throughout your presentation. Practice using your vocal tools to make the greatest impact regarding your message.

S – l – o – w D – o – w – n

Speaking too quickly causes several problems and is one of the most common voice mistakes. It can be both difficult to understand words spoken quickly and difficult to follow the logic of a presentation given at a super-fast pace.

One way to learn how to control your rate of speaking is to play around with it. Try saying a section of your presentation fast, then the next section slow. Vary your rate of speech in everyday conversation just to see how it feels. Take note of how quickly or slowly the people around you speak.

The rate of speech is a little like body language: It is not something most people think about regularly, and it tends to change with your moods and the situation. When you speak faster, you will be perceived as more excited. When you speak slower, you will be perceived as more serious. Being aware of your speaking pace is the first and most crucial step in learning to control it.

GPS Voice Technique©

Speeches are designed to be spoken, not written. You should not write and then memorize your speech. However, one tool that does require you to write out a section of your speech can be enormously helpful in practicing vocal techniques. It is **GPS (Giving Purposeful Speeches) Voice Technique**.

GPS Voice Technique uses symbols to provide visual indicators of how, when, and where to incorporate vocal rhythm to give emphasis to presentations. You write out a small section of your speech — perhaps an anecdote or one of your main points — then use the symbols, so you know where to include pauses, when to speak faster or slower, and when to speak louder or softer.

After practicing with one or two sections of your speech, you should apply those techniques to other parts but without writing it all out. The GPS Voice Technique symbols are simply an effective way to practice — *you still do not want to read your speech!*

Here are the symbols and examples of how you might use them for practice:

Pause	Speed	Volume
/ = 1-2 Seconds	_____ = Faster	↑ = Louder
// = 2-3 Seconds	-------- = Slower	↓ = Softer

Look at how these GPS symbols can change the meaning of your messages:

GPS Example A

  ↑   ↑

A woman / without her man / is nothing.

If you read this message as mapped, you may have to duck hurling objects thrown at your head! The rate of this sentence is fast. The volume goes up in the first two parts of the sentence. A short pause is given between two main parts. According to the meaning of how this sentence is mapped, the message implies a man defines a women's worth.

GPS Example B

↓   ↑

A woman // without her / man // is nothing.

Lead Out Loud!

If you read this message as mapped, you might receive a warm smile and supportive embrace. The sentence implies men are made whole by the magnificence of women. In scenario A, you might get kicked. In scenario B, you might get kissed!

Once you have all your symbols in place, play with reading your selection and using the symbols to direct your vocal variations. There is no one correct way. Correct is based on what message you want to convey. Say it in different ways to see which feels most comfortable. Deliver it to key people and ask them which way they feel works best based on your intended purpose. It can be a fun way to practice!

You have chosen an excellent topic. You have done enough research to discuss it authoritatively. You have prepared your first sentence, your main points, and your last sentence. You have created physical cues to help you stay on track. You have practiced gestures and developed a comfortable posture and stance. Using your voice to its fullest potential is the next step in delivering an outstanding presentation!

Phipps' Practice Tip

There are several useful ways to practice controlling your voice. You can call yourself, leave your speech on your voicemail, or use audio recordings. Listen for any inexplicable swells or drops that do not provide value.

Making recordings of yourself using the **GPS Voice Technique** can also be a useful way to learn more about vocal rhythm and volume. Just make sure you use it as a tool and not a crutch!

Since almost 40% of the impression formed by the audience about you is based on your voice; practice varying vocal techniques. Everyone has a vocal range. Make the most of yours!

Phipps' Voice Tip

**Avoid carbonated drinks before speaking.
On the other hand, if you burp during your speech;
you will be remembered.**

Speech Fillers

Identify Words that Negatively Impact Your Delivery

Since 93% of public speaking impact is nonverbal communication (55% body language and 38% voice), just how important is that remaining 7% of words? The answer is: It is huge!

Words alone can skyrocket or sink your messages. To ensure you avoid counterproductive words, be aware of the following energy thieves robbing you of your professional power!

Fillers

Definition: Words that unnecessarily fill in space between your words.

Purpose: Used as placeholders until you can think of what to say next.

Examples: *"um."*

Result: You sound unsure, timid, indecisive, or confused.

Solution: Pause between your statements.

**Most of us are oblivious to how often we use fillers.
Count the fillers you hear in one day.
You will probably get to 100 before lunch!**

Many people use fillers when speaking. You do not need them. Some people do not say "um" but say "ya know" or "and all." In normal conversation, fillers are less noticeable. When all the focus is on you, fillers become glaring. Count your "ums." You can either do that on your recording or ask a friend to count them for you as you speak. Remember, you cannot fix it until you find it.

Just reading this information about fillers will increase your awareness. You will start hearing unnecessary fillers from others more. If filler words are a huge problem for you, ask a friend to tell you each time you use one. Your brain will begin to train your mouth to avoid them.

Pausing will allow your audience's brains to catch up with your words. You will sound and feel more confident. When you pause during your speeches, allowing silence in your presentation, it gives the audience time to reflect and appreciate what you just said. Reducing or better yet, eliminating the fillers, will help you sound more confident.

> **Instead of speaking when there is an opportunity,
> speak when there is a need.**

Slang

> **Definition:** Deliberate modification of a standard word or phrase changing the meaning by developing a contrasting or alternative definition.
>
> **Purpose:** Demonstrate a casual, playful, and informal method of speaking.
>
> **Examples:** "Y'all," "that's cool," "you know," "I was like," "know what I'm saying," "seriously."
>
> **Result:** You sound unprofessional.
>
> **Solution:** Use specific wording.

Personally, I like slang. Appropriate slang highlights our diversity, our uniqueness, and can make us sound relevant to the generation or cultural group we are addressing. The perspective is, when you use inappropriate slang, you sound uneducated, disconnected, and outdated.

Take an innocent word such as "bad." If you avoided slang and told someone about the results of your last performance review, "My performance review was bad; I did not get the promotion," you are showing that you are disappointed. However, if you used slang, and told someone, "Man, I was *bad* in my performance review! I got the promotion!", you are excited. Your decision about how to describe your performance review will usually have something to do with whom you are talking — and so should your decision about when to use slang in a presentation!

In relaxed and casual settings, slang can help ease tension and make you appear more personable. In professional settings, here are common slang phrases to avoid:

- You know what I'm saying
- And then I was like
- Know what I mean
- Come on now
- But anyway
- This, that and the other
- Per se
- Things of that nature

A client asked me to conduct his coaching session at his home office. My client wanted to improve his public speaking skills by improving his grammar and reducing his slang.

He asked his son to leave the room so the coaching session could begin. He said, "Johnny, I gots to get da work. Get *somewheres* and do ya homework." The son replied, "I ain't got homework." My client looks at me and says,

Lead Out Loud!

"Son, *can't* you see the *talk* teacher is here, use proper English; It's "I ain't got <u>no</u> homework!"

Hards

Definition: Saying words such as "and," "so," and "but" loudly during transitional phrases.

Purpose: To hold your place in the conversation while thinking about your next thought.

Examples: "I went the store AND..." or "My alarm did not go off SO..."

Result: You sound unnecessarily explosive and as if you are struggling to complete a thought.

Solution: Avoid conjunctions by making two separate sentences. If you use conjunctions or hard words, say them at the consistent volume as the rest of the sentence.

These are "hard" words because when said mid-sentence, the volume goes up and it sounds like you are saying them *harder* than your other words. When we use "hards," we are unsure of what to say next. Using a "hard" tells the listener– "I am still talking; don't interrupt me." When you are presenting, it is unlikely the audience will interrupt, so using "hards" is particularly out of place and a bad habit.

Continuants

Definition: Words that unnecessarily continue a sentence.

Purpose: To prolong a statement, definition, or explanation.

Examples: "And," "because," "so," "therefore."

Result: You are perceived as rambling.

Solution: Avoid conjunctions. Use shorter sentences.

Here is a negative example- "Customer service is important BECAUSE we need to keep our clients happy AND show them we care BECAUSE ..." See how this sentence could go on too long? Here is a positive example- "Customer service is important. Let's show our customers we care. Focus on talking less and listening more." Can you see how this sentence is more concise?

Vagues

Definition: Indecisive, soft, or ambiguous words lacking measurable content.

Purpose: Casual efforts to demonstrate quantities for supportive information.

Examples: "Expensive," "soon," "most people," "famous," and "several."

Result: Can make you sound like you are exaggerating or lacking facts.

Solution: Use words with measurable content: dates, percentages, amounts, and specific times.

To establish credibility, use facts, not feelings. Verifiable facts are indisputable. Feelings are opinions and assumptions that can be based on facts — but are often vague. Using vagues makes you seem less reliable because they are ambiguous. Vague statements show up in informative conversations where facts would demonstrate experience and ability. See the comparison chart on the next page for examples.

Lead Out Loud!

Compare:

	VAGUES	FACTS
Experience	"Extensive research"	8 Years in Human Resources
Education	"Several courses"	Master's in Business Administration
Cost	"Very inexpensive"	$5.12 per Unit
Time	"ASAP"	All calls returned within 24 hours
Unnecessary Adverbs	"Basically" "Probably"	Actually, Usually

Words like "extensive," "several," or "inexpensive" are arguable. How much is "extensive"? How many are "several"? Ambiguity can result in negative deliberation in your audience. If your audience is busy deliberating, they are not paying attention. Under the facts column, the content is unquestionably clear. Strive to be factual when presenting; it will make you sound more professional.

Adapt to the Four Audience Types.

Different audiences may want the same information delivered in diverse ways. If you are presenting information about healthy eating to fifth graders, your technique may not be the same as if you are giving the same presentation to your co-workers. Part of the magic of being an effective speaker is knowing how to modify the delivery for the audience. Identifying the audience type is the first key.

Four Audience Types:

Efficient - want concise, clear, bottom-line information.

Emotional - want engaging, heart-warming messages.

Ease - want step-by-step and chronological information.

Expert - want detailed, analytical, thoroughly researched content.

	Efficient	Emotional	Ease	Expert
Prefer speakers who are	Brief Direct	Personable Interactive	Steady Organized	Accurate Proven
Prefer speakers who avoid	Rambling Details	Slow delivery	Inconsistency Rush delivery	Fabrication Ambiguity

In college, I sold vacuum cleaners. Although I did not know a lot about vacuum cleaners, I had success because I figured out how to adapt my sales pitch to each of my customer's styles. If I had an Efficient Audience, I showed how quickly the machine cleaned and how easy it was to assemble. For an Emotional Audience, I demonstrated the many attachments and told stories of how much time you could save by cleaning less and playing more. If I had an Ease Audience, I emphasized the longevity of the company and showed evidence of its award-winning customer service. When I had an Expert Audience, I would conduct a side-by-side comparison with their current vacuum cleaner, followed by showing high scores from sources in consumer reports.

The general manager asked how I sold so many vacuum cleaners. I was not a vacuum expert. My success was in adapting my approach to the audience type of my prospective customer.

Whether you are in sales, management, information technology, manufacturing, politics, or education, being able to recognize your audience type will be useful. Regardless of the audience type, your content will remain consistent, but adaptations to suit your audience should be flexible. Boring, snoring, and ignoring are the words that many speakers worry will describe the audience's experience. Get over it!

> **You cannot control what your audiences think.**
> **You can control what you give your**
> **audiences to think about.**

Use Public Speech Engagers to Connect with Your Audiences.

When you cook, salt and pepper are common seasonings. Content and research are the salt and pepper to a presentation. When you want to spice up your foods, you add cayenne pepper, paprika, oregano, or garlic. When you want to spice up your presentations, you add speech seasoning beyond the basic salt and pepper facts.

To add spice, flavor, and overall interest to your presentations, there are four types of approaches called "Public Speech Engagers (PSE)." Just like spices enhance the taste of food, the Public Speech Engagers boost the interest level of your presentations. Public Speech Engagers are tools you can incorporate to add interest, illustrate messages, or validate points.

Four types of speech engagers:

- Questions
- Quotes
- Statistics
- Stories

	Efficient	Emotional	Ease	Expert
Questions	Direct	Imaginative	Realistic	Analytical
Quotes	Successful	Funny	Historical	Renowned
Statistics	Results	Relatable	Personable	Quantifiable
Stories	Short	Entertaining	Orderly	Accurate

Experiment using each type. Figure out what will work best for your purposes. Public Speech Engagers are a fantastic way to capture and hold your audience's attention. Like spices in cooking, use PSE with care!

During the preparation of your presentation, decide which of the four public speech engagers will best serve your purpose. As you practice polishing your body language and vocal techniques, you may find you need to practice incorporating these techniques more than other parts of your speech. If you have ever botched telling a joke or a story, you know what I am talking about.

Public Speech Engagers require practice and timing. They are more powerful when combined with other techniques such as modifying body language, voice inflections, and word usage. If you pause for one or two seconds before and after you give a Public Speech Enhancer, you arouse audience interest, you emphasize it, and you give the audience a moment to "digest" what you said.

Lead Out Loud!

The pause just before delivering is an auditory transition letting your audience know you are about to illustrate a point. The pause after allows what you said to register. Besides building interest, pauses will help you stay focused and make your presentation more enjoyable to deliver and to hear.

Experiment using PSE at the beginning, middle, and end of your speeches. Vary how and when you use them. Your great story may work better as an opening than as a close. A relevant statistic might work in the middle of your speech as a comparative tool. You may want to close with a quote that solidifies your entire message. You may want to use questions throughout the presentation to keep your audience engaged. There is no one right way to use a Public Speech Enhancer. Although each type has specific rules, it is up to you to decide when you use them.

Rules of Using Public Speech Engagers

Questions

- Ask questions that intrigue and make your audience think.
- Use questions containing the words, "what," or "how."
- Avoid asking multiple questions back to back.
- Acknowledge the answers if questions are non-rhetorical.
- Keep questions clear of confusing or negative wording.
- Sparingly use "*How many of you...?*" questions, because this only result in a hand raise without intriguing or fully engaging your audience. Instead of asking your audience, "Do you like to travel?" ask them, "What is your favorite place to visit?"

Quotes

- Use the person's full name.

- State their relevant credentials.

- Say exactly what they said without embellishment or paraphrase.

- Avoid using, "*A famous person once said*...." If they are famous, you should know their name. Instead say, "*According to Michael Jordan, six-time Finals Most Valuable Player in the National Basketball Association, said, "I can handle losing, I cannot handle not trying."*

Statistics

- Use quantifiable and measurable data (numbers, dates, times, percentages).

- Cite the source.

- Avoid vague statistics such as, "4 out of 5 doctors recommend". Instead say, "According to Erlanger Hospital in Chattanooga, TN, a Top 100 Hospital in the United States, 80% of neurosurgeons suggest yoga strengthens the back."

Stories

- Make your story or stories only about 20% of your total talk time.

- Keep your story's content relevant to your message.

- Use personal experiences. Share life lessons. All are great ways to use storytelling maintain interest. Stories do not have to be long, funny, or motivational. Stories should be relevant.

Practice

Does practice make perfect? No! Practice can make improvements. You cannot improve unless you practice. However, if what you practice is consistently wrong, you will waste time and get poor or no results. However, you can practice smart, be efficient, get results faster, and have increased content retention. First, let's address common practice mistakes.

Mistake #1: Writing the entire speech.

Stop writing your speeches. You will spend more time erasing or deleting than speaking. It is OK to use the outline but avoid multi-page outlines.

Mistake #2: Only practicing mentally.

Stop saying your speech only in your head without saying it aloud. In your head, your mouth never gets dry, your lungs are always strong, and your voice is immaculate. When speaking aloud: air, endurance, and timing tremendously affect delivery.

Mistake #3: Being afraid of practice.

Stop thinking, "I may over-practice!" That is only an excuse to justify avoiding practice. If you have practiced so much that your speech is boring to you, try:

- Varying the delivery.
- Switching around your public speech engagers.
- Telling it sitting down versus standing up.
- Telling it in reverse.

Whenever someone asks me, "How long should I practice?" My answer is always, "Practice until you replace your anxiety with anticipation."

**The difference between mediocre and magnificent
is the passion for improving.**

You should practice three ways:

> **Live Audience-** Practice in front of picky people you trust will be honest with you. Ask them to be your audience. They will usually say, "*Yes!*" If you can please picky people, you can please a sympathetic audience that wants you to do well.

> **Video Record-** Use a video camera to record your presentation. Replay it with the audio turned off. Observe your body language and facial expressions and make improvements where necessary.

> **Audio Record-** Use a video or audio recorder focusing only on your vocals. Concentrate on hearing your voice. Make improvements to various aspects of your tone such as your volume, rate of speaking, and making appropriate pauses.

Each time you practice, deliver your presentation differently. Variation will help you develop confidence and sound more conversational. Varying your presentation order can also cement your main points in your mind.

In the initial stages of preparation, practice following your speech outline, create physical cues, practice the delivery of Public Speech Engagers, and experiment with adaptations for different audience types. Remember to incorporate body language, vocal variations, and the use of content. Practice until your presentation becomes polished and professional. Practice various techniques, so you are comfortable with yourself and your material by the time you give your speech.

My mother served 28 years in the United States Army. I asked her why soldiers prepared so hard in training. She told me, "The more they bleed in training, the less they bleed in combat."

Lead Out Loud!

Phipps' Practice Tip

As you practice, try moving your speech engagers to see where they work best. Combine specific movements with speech engagers to see if the body language changes the impact of the enhancer.

You should also experiment with changing your rate of speech and volume when making use of speech engagers. The **GPS Voice Technique** and speech engagers work well together because the engagers are usually easy to write out and map.

Modern technology is convenient. Wireless communication and voice recognition software is not just the future; it is the now! Your presentation skills must remain strong despite the use of this technology. Some speakers will use PowerPoint. If you use it, here are tips:

- Use six, simple lines per slide, or less.
- Avoid looking at the screen while talking.
- Use pictures or images instead of text-heavy slides.
- Provide a handout of the slides with speaker notes (main points).

You cannot text your way through a speech. You cannot email your way through a presentation. The words you use and the way you use them will tell your audience your level of preparation and professionalism. Use the words that best reflect you and your messages.

Procrastination means you will do it tomorrow.
Dedication means you will do it forever.

Miscellaneous Tips:

- Enter with confidence.
- Speak with clarity.
- If you lose your place, keep going!

- Being nervous is OK. Look and sound confident.
- Ask "what" or "how" questions to engage.
- Get comfortable with being uncomfortable.
- If you are happy to be there, look like it!
- Practice until you replace anxiety with eagerness.
- Conclude with competence.

Three Reasons Your Presentations are Boring

Want your audience to stop looking at their watches and start watching you? Then make sure you stop doing the following four things that bore your audiences and rob you of your professional power!

1. Boring Beginnings

"Hello, I am happy to be here today..." or "OK, I have a few things to cover, and I'll be brief ..." are boring starts to what often become yawn festivals. When your audience hears these canned beginnings, their brains go into "here we go again" mode, and they shut down. Here are a few ways to avoid a boring beginning:

- Begin with an activity.
- Create a quiz.
- Break the audience into small groups.
- Start with an intriguing question that requires your audience to think.

Beginning in an unusual, active way allows for quick networking, builds rapport, and generates energy. When everyone regroups, they get wired up and ready to listen to you!

2. Monotone Voice

Before you say anything bad or good about your voice, remember that you can always talk faster, slower, louder, or softer.

Lead Out Loud!

No matter how you normally sound, if you do not vary your volume, speed, and tone, you will sound boring. Say certain phrases faster to show excitement. Say certain words or phrases slower for serious emphasis. Pause two or three seconds for dramatic effect. Let your voice be an instrument of influence.

3. Speech Reading

If you were going to use note cards, PowerPoint slides, or a script, just save everyone time and money by emailing your speech and stay home. As children, our parents read us stories when they wanted us to go to sleep. As adults, when read to, we get sleepy! If your presentation is content-heavy, tell your audience they can contact you for more detail. You can also offer to send details or content-heavy slides to them as a bonus.

Don't memorize your presentation. Learn it!

Prepare for Presentation Excellence

Before **Your Next Speech:**

- Identify your purpose.
- Ask about your timeline.
- Develop your speech outline.
- Solidify your topic into one main point.
- Include sub-points for continuity.
- Decide on opening and closing statements.
- Know the first and last words you want to say to develop structure.
- Give fewer details if your speech needs to be shorter.
- Add content if you will be speaking longer.

Phipps' Practice Tip

Give your speech in the shower. Tell it to your friends. Leave it on your voicemail. Share it while standing in line. Say it before going to sleep. Give it first thing in the morning. Make it your kid's bedtime story. Ask your significant other to critique you. Practice until you replace your anxiety with anticipation.

During Your Next Speech:

- Arrive early to alleviate the stress created by running late.
- Arrive early enough to check out the room.
- Know the timeframe.
- Bring material.
- Bring backups.
- Check the equipment.
- Be hygienic.
- Greet guests.
- Use names.
- Introduce yourself.
- Record yourself.
- Video or audio record.
- Ask a friend to take pictures.
- Begin a log of your presentations.
- Capture key ideas said during the moment.

Remember, keep going! Someone may spill a glass of water. A phone may ring. Someone may be typing or texting. Someone may sneeze. Someone may be talking to someone else. You may say point No. 2 then forget No. 3 and skip to No. 4. The microphone may go out. The projection screen or next slide may malfunction. You are the speaker, and the audience is there for you. Be there for them. Keep going.

After Your Next Speech:

- Pay attention to your recordings.
- Observe your body language.
- Listen to your voice.
- Take note of your content. The more selective you are now, the better you will be later.
- Request feedback.
- Evaluate performance.

I recommend the **Keep-Stop-Start** method. It helps when you want feedback without asking several questions:

- **Keep** What should I **Keep** doing?
- **Stop** What should I **Stop** doing?
- **Start** What should I **Start** doing?

Most audiences are sympathetic. They want you to do well. A sympathetic audience admires those who have the courage to be the speaker. Some pessimists or insecure people can present challenges for you as the speaker. Put them back in their place by properly preparing and presenting.

Speaking is a gift. Most fear it and even more run from it. The ability to present yourself effectively with confidence and competence will give you an advantage. No matter who you are, society has a reason you should fail. You may be too old. You may be too young. Your waist may not be the typical size. You may live in a different ZIP code. Your hair (if you have hair) may look different.

Set yourself positively apart from others by being able to express yourself successfully and skillfully. Embrace your inner speaker. You have a right to be heard. You do not need to be the best speaker; just be better.

Remember the Fundamentals

Technology has changed how we communicate. The ability to effectively demonstrate interpersonal communication with clarity and confidence is vital.

> My great-grandmother asked my grandmother, "Why don't you visit more often?" My grandmother said, "Nobody travels out to the country anymore. I will write you letters instead." My grandmother asked my mother, "Why don't you write more often?" My mother said, "Nobody writes letters *anymore*. I will call you on the telephone instead." My mother asked me, "Why don't you call me anymore?" I said, "Nobody calls on the telephone anymore. I will send you an email." I asked my daughter, "Why don't you email me anymore?" She said, "Nobody emails anymore. I will text you." My daughter asked her friends, "Why didn't you return my text message?" Her friends said, "I replied on Social Media."

What is happening to our willingness to be around other people? What happened to our ability to give an interview without needing a computer in our hand, lap, or in our phones? What happened to our skill level that we are unable to approach a podium without note cards? What happened to our networking skills that it takes us three minutes to tell someone what we do for a living? Public speaking is more than a professional development skill. Being able to convey a message effectively gives you an advantage that others lack.

Let your actions be your evidence.

Even if you are a genius, with years of experience, possessing both the academic and professional pedigree, if you speak with

Lead Out Loud!

low confidence and minimal conviction, you will miss opportunities to get full credit for being the professional you have worked hard to become.

Be your best self when speaking. Avoid trying to mimic or fabricate someone else's speaking style. Your best you is your genuine you. Remember, no one will trust your message until they first trust you.

**Leave every room in a better condition
than when you entered.**

Chapter 4:
Just Spit It Out -
Communication Keys
for Success

Importance of Listening

Our most important yet least trained communication skill is listening. We all can be continual learners, but unless you have the proper content taught to you in the way you can best receive it, it can be challenging to learn properly.

> My first mind modification moment of listening was an epiphany I owe to my daughter, Taylor. When she was ten, Taylor, like every awesome granddaughter, loved her Grandpa. My father's greatest joys on Earth are his love of piloting his airplane and his love for his grandbaby! When my dad can fly his airplane and be with Taylor, the energy from his smile could light up a medium-sized city!
>
> Dad asked could Taylor and he go flying on Saturday morning. My daughter overheard the conversation and immediately got excited, "Is that grandpa? Are we going flying? Can I fly the plane this time? Tell grandpa I paid attention last time. I know which buttons not to push!"
>
> I told Taylor, "Yes, Baby. You can go flying with Grandpa. But first, clean up your room, make your bed, and brush your teeth." I felt these were reasonable requests. I sent my daughter upstairs. About 30 minutes passed. I hear my father driving up to the house. The sound of my daughter rocketing out of her room shook the floor! She is fully dressed, her hair is beautiful, and she is wearing her "Grandpa's co-pilot t-shirt."
>
> As the two of them exit, I calmly ask, "Baby, did you clean your room, make your bed, and brush your teeth?" Without even turning around she yells, "Yes Sir, pretty much!" I see dad opening the door for Taylor, and they begin to drive away. Of course, every father knows you

should trust your children. I am fond of the sentiments made by former President Ronald Reagan about the Soviet Union, "Trust but Verify."

So, I went upstairs to verify! Soccer shoes and dresses covered her room. Her bed was lumpy, and her toothbrush was dry. I raced back downstairs and could still see my dad's truck down the street. I began yelling and waving. My Dad drove back to the house. As Taylor got out of the car, I belted, "Get your butt upstairs! You are not going anywhere until that room is clean! You never listen!"

My dad, as usual, remained composed and just sat on the couch. He said, "Do what your father said. I'll be right here until you finish." Taylor dragged herself upstairs crying and complaining at the same time. At the top of the stairs, she turns and utters, "Dad, may I say something?" I angrily responded, "What is it?" Taylor said, "If you say I am a bad listener, and you teach people how to listen, then that means you are a bad teacher!"

I have asked over 10,000 managers how well they felt they listened. The answers varied from, "Well, it depends," "Pretty Good," "Lousy," etc. I wanted to acquire more quantifiable data to assess the accuracy of our listening skills. I changed my question. I started asking instead, "If you had to give yourself a listening score, ranging from 0 – 100%, with 100% being a perfect listener, what score would you give yourself of how well you feel you listen?

The average number given was 75%. No one has ever told me 100%! Based on these results, I created a listening test. The test is on video. Although the video is only about 60 seconds, it measures how well a person listens using the two hemispheres of the brain. The left side listens for logical content that is measurable such as numbers, dates, times, names, and percentages. The right side of your brain listens for emotional content that is non-measurable such as volume, body language, and facial expressions.

The test has ten questions. The first five questions measure left side, logical, content listening. The last five questions measure right side, emotional, nonverbal listening. When given the test, participants can only answer about two or three questions. After showing this video and testing thousands of professionals of all demographics, our results showed, although the average person feels they listen at 75%, they only average a score of 25%. When you improve your listening skills, you improve your communication skills.

There are four dynamics in which we communicate:

1. Writing: note taking, typing, texting, scribbling, journaling, etc. The average professional spends approximately twelve years learning how to write, yet they spend only 9% of their day writing. Even when taking notes, we usually skip words, use abbreviations, and miss important content.

2. Reading: books, articles, the internet, instructions, manuals, etc. The average professional spends approximately nine years learning how to read, yet they spend only 16% of their day reading. The word "skimming" is becoming increasingly popular. Skimming is another way of saying, "I by no means read it. I did look at a few pages and can acknowledge the existence of the material. I have no clue about the full content information."

3. Speaking: face-to-face, meetings, telephone, networking, presentations, etc. The average professional spends approximately one year learning how to be a more effective speaker. The average person speaks for 35% of their day. Even when taken as a collegiate course, the average time of a semester class is 3.5 months.

4. Listening: Understanding and recalling shared information. The average professional receives little to no training on how to be a better listener.; yet the average person listens 40% of their day.

Let's review!

	Years of Study	% Used Daily
Reading	12 Years	9%
Writing	7 Years	16%
Speaking	0 - 1 Year	35%
Listening	0 Years	40%

There is an inverse correlation between the amount of time we invest in learning a communication skill, to the amount of time we spend using that skill. In other words, the more of that skill we need, the less training we receive on learning how to use it effectively. This is the reason I decided to create strategies and approaches addressing our most important, yet least trained communication skill—listening.

Three Dynamics of Listening:
- **Acknowledge** – Pay attention.
- **Gather** – Ask for information.
- **Observe** – Recognize non-verbal.

When it comes to listening, most of us do one or maybe two of these areas well. The challenge is unless we are proficient in all three areas, it increases the susceptibility of making communication mistakes. The following will examine all three dynamics of listening in addition to specific techniques you can incorporate where needed to increase your communication efficiency.

Acknowledge

1. **Acknowledge:** Focusing on the other person. We acknowledge the speaker by establishing two elements:
    a. **Eye Contact**: Looking at the other person while you are listening to them.

Eye contact is important to show respect and enables us to ascertain additional, unspoken information from the other person's body language and facial expressions. My parents told me to always look a person in the eye to show respect. In American culture, this may be universal. Internationally, eye contact may be disrespectful or even aggressive. My recommendation is when in American culture, maintain your eye contact to let the other person know you are focused on them. Looking at the other person also gives you a chance to identify their subconscious thoughts by how they react in their facial expressions and body language.

    b. **Continual Comments**: Continuing conversational flow and keeping them talking.

Continual Comments are more like grunts and murmurs rather than words. These are verbal acknowledgments we insert when listening to others. Continual comments tell the other person, "Continue talking; I am still listening." It makes the other person feel what they are saying has value when they consistently hear your responses.

Always maintain eye contact when using Continual Comments. Also, use slow head nods. Look for strategic moments to insert Continual Comments. Using them repetitiously without variation can be annoying. However, using a variety, during breaks in the conversation, can make the gestures seem more genuine.

Examples of Continual Comments:

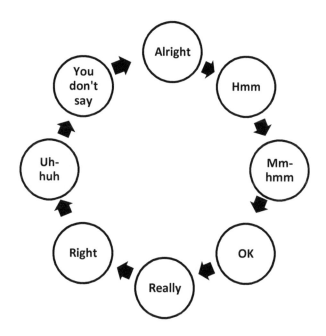

Acknowledge- Show You are Actively Listening

Eye Contact

- Provides visual information.
  - Shows courtesy.
  - Builds rapport.

Continual Comments

- Gets more verbal information.
- Continues the conversation.
  - Engages the speaker.

117

Gather

Confirming Understanding

The person asking the questions controls the conversation. An effort to ask questions shows your interest in wanting to learn more. Great leaders, great conversationalists, and great decision makers have something in common; they ask questions to relate and not just to debate.

We should ask questions to get more information while we are listening. We should ask the questions to either broaden our current understanding, get new data, or to gain an understanding of the other person's perspective before refuting their point of view. Violating the following six guidelines for questions stifles good efforts to communicate:

Six Guidelines for Questions:

1. Know what you want to know.

Determine if you need continuation, confirmation, clarification, or more information. Asking better question gets you better answers. Decide if you want your question to generate discussion with longer answers or solidify information with shorter answers.

2. Ask one question at a time.

What happens when you are asked multiple questions back, to back, to back? "What do you like about your job, and if you like it, what is your favorite part, and why did you choose that career field?" Too many questions at once can be confusing for the listener. In a series of multiple questions, which gets answered, the first question, the last question, the question they remember, the question they know the answer to? Keep it simple by asking one question then allow them to answer.

3. Pause to allow for an answer.

Extroverted people (Dominant and Energetic styles–see Leadership Chapter 2) are more likely to ask a question, then interrupt the speaker. Avoid this mistake regardless of your leadership and personality style. It is harder to get smarter if you are talking. The best way to get additional information is to ask better questions and allow time for the other person to respond.

4. Keep questions short.

After asking a question, avoid re-asking, using an analogy, telling a story, or asking another question. Short questions require more thought. It is easier to ramble convoluted thoughts hoping the other person will decipher what you mean and provide a quality answer. Be sure to have a definitive close after your questions to let the other person know you are anticipating an answer. Keep your questions under ten words. Shorter questions increase the likelihood of a more sustainable answer.

5. Make questions clear.

Avoid the word "not" and double negatives in your questions. It makes the answer confusing. Here are examples of poorly asked "not" questions that even when answered, the answer is still unclear:

- Are you not in agreement?
- Don't you understand?
- Is it not?

If the answer to each question was "Yes," is the answer clear? What if the answer to each question was "no," is the answer clear? Regardless, if the answer is "no" or "yes," it is still confusing. The solution to making questions clearer is to remove the word "not" from

119

Lead Out Loud!

those negative questions.

- Are you in agreement?
- Do you understand?
- Is it?

Whether the answer to these questions is "no" or "yes," the answer has more clarity.

6. Qualify your questions.

Context is a key component to questions. Asking a person, "Which way is best?" is a different question than asking, "Regarding the instructions given, which way is best?"

When we hear answer-oriented words such as: what, when, how, and who; we begin formulating a response. If additional information continues to come after the question, our brains are forced to stop, reprocess, and gather more information. To best communicate, place supportive information before to qualify the question.

Four Types of Questions

Closed vs. Open Questions

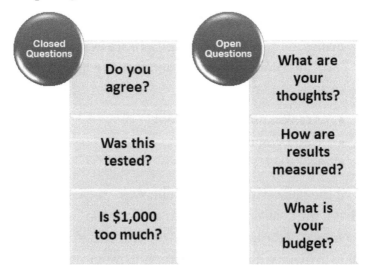

Clarity Questions

Clarity questions are designed to get you an answer to an unanswered question. Let's say you want to know how much a potential client can afford. You may ask the following question, "How much can your company afford?" If they answer, "Well, we have a limited budget right now." Notice how they responded but did not answer. If you were to repeat yourself and ask that question again, they might reply, "Like I said, we don't have a whole lot in our budget."

Even if you have the best of intentions, if your repertoire of questions is limited, you will be unable to ascertain needed information to help others or advance resolutions. People will prevent answering your questions for various reasons:

- They may be unwilling to answer.
- They may be unable to answer.
- They may be without an answer.
- They may be too confused to answer.

Each word has an average of six definitions. When you ask for their "budget," they may think you want to know their maximum amount, and they want to prevent being taken advantage of. In contrast, when you ask for their "budget," you want to know what they can allocate so you provide them the best service you know they can afford.

Here is how you use the Clarity Question Technique to get a clear answer to an unanswered question:

Step One - Ask an Open Question.

How much can your company afford?

Step Two - Identify the initial questions keywords, (usually the nouns and verbs).

How much can your company afford?

Lead Out Loud!

Keywords:

- company
- afford

Step Three: Find at least three alternatives/synonyms for each of the keywords.

Keywords:

- **company:** organization, team, department, firm, decision makers
- **afford:** budget, allocate, range, come up with, feel comfortable, amount

Step Four: Re-ask the same type of question replacing the keywords with the alternatives.

- How much can your company afford?
- What amount range is the organization comfortable with?
- Regarding the budget of your decision makers, what is allocated?

Here is another example

Step One: Ask an Open Question.

What are your thoughts about this idea?

Step Two: Identify the keywords.

What are your thoughts about this idea?

Keywords:

- thoughts
- idea

Step Three: Find alternatives.

Keywords:

- **thoughts:** feelings, opinions, views, perspectives

- **idea:** plan, suggestion, strategy, proposal, approach

Step Four: Re-ask.

- How do you feel about this approach?
- Regarding this strategy, what is your opinion?
- Since this is a new suggestion, what are your views on its success?

If you have yet to receive an answer asking at least three Clarity Questions, stop asking. A person who has yet to answer after asked three questions, either does not have the answer or does not want to divulge that information at that time. It is best to stop asking and move on. The Clarity Question works well when the other person is willing to communicate, yet their answers are ambiguous. Questions types at the top of the pyramid will garner more information.

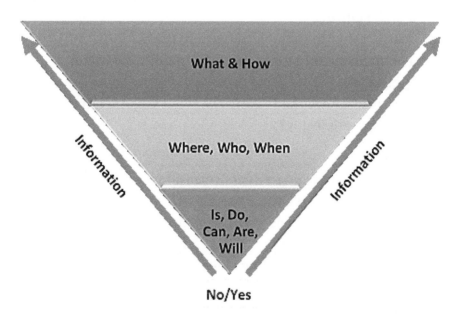

Lead Out Loud!

Connector Questions

Connector Questions are designed to continue the flow of conversations by asking questions connecting key points.

Steps for using Connector Questions

Step One: Ask an Open Question
Step Two: Listen for keywords said by the other person.
Step Three: Ask another open question using one of the keywords used by the other person.

Example #1

You: What do you do for fun?
Them: I like to **travel**?
You: Wow! So, which places have been your favorite to **travel**?
Them: **Germany** was gorgeous. I love the **food**, the **music**, and the **culture**.
You: What is an example of German food?
Them: Schnitzel is a popular **dish**. However, my **wife** is **vegetarian**.
You: I have never had **Schnitzel**. What **vegetarian dishes** did your **wife** enjoy?

Example #2

You: What are your areas of professional expertise?
Them: I am a **marketing specialist**.
You: Marketing is a needed skill. Which are the areas in which you **specialize**?
Them: I focus on **branding** for **small** to **medium** sized **businesses**.
You: What have been some challenges with working with **smaller businesses**?
Them: Usually they have great **ideas** but **limited budgets**.

You: How do you turn great **ideas** into workable plans if they have a **limited budget**?

When using Connector Questions, the goal is to establish rapport and allow the other person to share. The Connector Question is your opportunity show concern and interest.

Review- Four Types of Questions

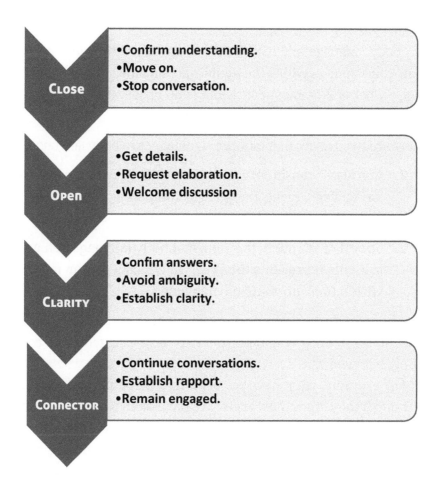

Close
- Confirm understanding.
- Move on.
- Stop conversation.

Open
- Get details.
- Request elaboration.
- Welcome discussion

Clarity
- Confim answers.
- Avoid ambiguity.
- Establish clarity.

Connector
- Continue conversations.
- Establish rapport.
- Remain engaged.

Lead Out Loud!

Observe

Recognizing Nonverbals – Body Language and Voice

Nonverbal communication makes up approximately 93% of communication. Two dynamics encapsulate Nonverbal communication: Body Language (55%) and Voice (38%). When you increase the awareness of the nonverbal communication; you increase your propensity for intuition, making you a more effective communicator.

Observe Body Language

Body language and its indicators can vary. Although there are some consistencies within the significance and meaning of body language, what will be most consistent is an observation of that person's normal nonverbal communication.

There are two factors that indicate significance in body language:

1. **Change**- Transition in their normal body language behavior. This represents the changes compared to what they normally do.

2. **Speed** -The rate in their normal body language behavior. This represents the speed in which a person moves within their normal body language.

Although there is some scientific merit that validates certain movements in body language, there are also exaggerations commonly believed as true.

For example, what have we been told is the person's feeling or mood if they cross their arms? We have been told the meaning of crossed arms indicates: defensiveness, not listening, or disinterest. Yet, a person with crossed arms could also stand or sit that way because they are comfortable. Another example is, touching your face while you are speaking means you are lying. It could also

126

mean that you face was itching while you were speaking.

It can become easy to associate a person's movement with meaning quickly. Some indicators are more distinguishable than others. For example, if a person rolls their eyes immediately after saying a person's name, it may indicate contempt for that person. If a person starts shaking their head up and down, then they start smiling, it may indicate they what they are hearing is favorable. Each body language movement may only have significance to that individual.

> One of my mother's favorite television shows was Magnum P.I. This was a 1980's show starring Tom Selleck, who played a handsome private investigator with a perfect mustache. My father disliked the show or most likely, disliked my mother enjoying looking at Tom Selleck. To regain what my father thought was lost attention, my father attempted to grow a perfect Tom Selleck mustache. Although it was a valiant effort, my father's mustache never reached the robustness of Tom Selleck's. During each episode, when my parents watched the show, my father would rub his mustache. The more my mother smiled at the T.V. screen, the more my father would rub his mustache. Today, over 30 years later, my father now has a smooth face. When my father gets irritated today, he rubs his upper lip. If I rub my lip or if you rub your lip, it may have little significance. However, when my father rubs his lip, he is probably angry!

Although each body language indicator can be unique, there are some movements in body language that have stronger indicators based on human physiology.

Eye Contact

Eye contact is usually a sign of respect or interest. Eye contact

127

becomes a stare when the person giving the eye contact does not blink or nod their head. To increase awareness of communication significance, be sure to look at the other person when they are speaking. Make special attention to the eyes of the other person.

Eye Movement

Eye movement can indicate significance in that person's train of thought. Although you may be unaware of what they are exactly thinking, by watching their eyes, you can get an idea of how they are processing their current information.

By looking at the eye positioning of the other person, it can give us insights on how they are mentally processing their information. The following directions are based on what you will see when you are focusing on the speaker. It is consistent in all genders, ages, and races. It is also consistent whether you are left or right handed.

Looking Up

When a person looks up, it can mean they are pondering their next thought. At this point, remain silent by pausing. Allow the other person to culminate what they are thinking. Even if you feel you are contributing to the conversation, you should remain quiet to enable them to complete their thought.

Looking Down

When a person looks down, it can mean they are ashamed of what they are saying or doubt the validity of what they are saying. When you see a person looking down, you should lower your tone and talk slower. Too much verbal bombardment at this point could be emotional and informational overload. When people get too emotional, they become horrible listeners.

Looking Up and to Their Left

When a person looks up and to their left, they are recalling visual information. Technically, it is when they look up and to their left, 45 degrees from a horizontal plane. The left side of the brain is connected to the brain's optic nerve. This nerve is galvanizing the portion of the brain that facilitates visual recollection. In other words, when the eyes go up and to the left at an angle, it is like hitting the rewind button. When you see someone doing this, they are speaking from either past experiences or regurgitating information from something they have personally seen.

Looking Up and to Their Right

When a person looks up and to their right, they are creating information. As with the left side, this is the case when the eyes look up and to the right, 45 degrees from the horizontal plane. This triggers the portion of the brain responsible for creativity and imagination. When you see a person doing this, they are speaking from the point of view where they are creating the information while they are speaking.

Those who exaggerate the significance of non-verbal physiological science inaccurately assume a person looking up and to the left, to be honest, and someone looking up and to the right as a liar. This is a misuse and over-generalization of the science. Although the science is valid, true or false is based on the context of the conversation.

For example, if you ask a person, "How can this problem be solved?" Let's say the person responding, before answering you, looks up and to the right, then answers. According to the science, that tells us that their answer is originating from a place of creativity. If the problem is new, the solution may yet to exist. Therefore, to resolve the issue, it may require a new, innovative, and creative approach.

Now let's say, you ask a different question such as, "I have been trying to reach you the last six hours. Where have you been? Let's say the person responding, before answering you, looks up and to their right, then answers. According to the science, this person is fabricating and creating answers.

Observe Voice

Voice is not an exact science. The significance is indicated by the individual's change in speed compared to their baseline normal behavior. For discrepancy inconsistencies request clarification.

Listen for:

- **Changes in volume** - Loud volume may indicate excitement. Softer volume may indicate seriousness.
- **Changes in speed**. - A fast speed may indicate excitement. A slower speed could indicate seriousness.
- **Use of fillers** - such as uh, um, ah, like, so, etc. More use of fillers could indicate nervousness and uncertainty, and less use of filler could indicate confidence and certainty.

**Communication is *not the* message you send;
Communication is the message understood.**

CHAPTER CHALLENGE

Ask at least three open questions before giving recommendations or advice.

CHAPTER 5:
When the Spit Hits the Fan
– The Art of
Conflict Resolution

Lead Out Loud!

After effectively listening to others, the next element of communication is responding. Although we cannot dictate what others may think, based on our responses, we can have an impact on the conversational flow.

Facts vs. Feeling

That's a fact! Or is it? One of the best ways to avoid conflicts is to avoid using statements of opinion and use more statements of fact.

Our company's research tells us that based on the statements made by the average person, 92% are opinionated and 8% are factual. A statement of opinion is different than a statement of fact. This is also true of a statement of facts versus a statement of truth. Truth is more of a perspective or viewpoints. Factual statements are rooted in quantifiable data. This data includes some form of numbers or specific information such as amounts, dates, times, quantities, and percentages.

For example, if you are walking outside in Las Vegas Nevada, during July, you may say, "It's hot." Although that statement may be true to you, it is an opinion. If someone were to say, "The temperature is 102 degrees." This is a statement of fact based on data.

Avoid misunderstandings by knowing the difference between making statements of fact, which contains non-opinionated and quantifiable data, versus making statements of feelings which contain opinionated and emotional data.

	Statements of Fact	**Statements of Feelings**
Rules	Requires numbers, percentages, times, names, dates, and measurable data.	Used to share perception, opinion, viewpoint, and personal insight.

	Statement of Facts	Statement of Feelings
	The cost is $2,221.	This is too expensive.
Examples	Adam arrived at 9:14 a.m.	She was very late.
	The approval rating is 96%.	All our clients love us.

Here are more examples:

Topic	Factual	Opinion
Weather	We received 8 inches of rain.	It has been an ugly day.
Movies	Titanic won 11 academy awards.	This film was great!
Finance	The U.S. employment rate is 4.9%.	The economy is steady.
Sports	115 million people watched Super Bowl.	Football is popular.

If you can argue it, disagree with it, or debate it, it is usually an opinion. Although some people will challenge anything, statements containing quantifiable data (numbers) can be harder to argue. Avoid conflicts by replacing opinionated statements with quantifiable data void of emotion.

The following statements may be true:

- She arrived late.
- They are angry with us.
- What they are asking for is too expensive.

Look at examples of how to reword these potentially emotionally charged statements by using statements of facts:

Lead Out Loud!

- The meeting started at 2:00 p.m. Janet arrived at 2:12 p.m.
- Mr. Smith left a four-minute voice mail requesting an explanation.
- Our budget is $1,000. The asking price $3,500.

Our opinions have value. Based on our expertise, background, and level of education, some opinions are held in higher regard than others. During moments of conflict or potential miscommunication, strive to be informative.

F.I.X. Problems

Others may forget their mistakes, but they may remember the pain of the correction. Even if you do your part of addressing the problem and offering a resolution, if the person corrected feels chastised or belittled, they will have reduced personal accountability.

Here is an old-school example of a typical correction: ©

Manager: *I wanted to talk with you about the filing system.*

Employee: *O.K.*

Manager: *You placed the client files in the wrong order.*

Employee: *I see.*

Manager: *You caused errors that you will need to fix.*

Employee: *I did?*

Manager: *Look into it and fix it.*

Employee: *All right.*

Manager: *Glad we had this discussion. Let's get back to work.*

Employee: *Fine.*

How much buy-in did the employee have? What questions did the employee ask the manager? What is the employee to resolve?

134

How well did the manager get feedback from the employee?

There are a plethora of errors with this type of correction. The good news is, at least they addressed the issue. Both the employee and the manager may want a favorable outcome. The challenge is, they addressed the issue but did not implement a correction.

Being an effective leader requires an element of being able to correct others effectively. The following is a technique called, **F.I.X.** It is a corrective technique that addresses three essential elements of a correction:

1. Clarify what happened.

2. State expectations.

3. Discuss solutions.

The F.I.X. represents three components:

Step One: **F** - Find out what happened by asking questions.

Step Two: **I** - Inform everyone of the expectations.

Step Three: **X** -Examine solutions by asking questions.

Most of us do well at informing others of their mistakes. This is step two. Often a correction begins with step two. This is a flaw in leadership and communication. We must start with first asking for clarity. A correction should start with the following type of question:

- What happened?

- How did this occur?

- What caused it?

If you are a Task Style (Dominant or Analytical, see Chapter 2), resist the temptation of surpassing Step One. Start by asking questions to gain an understanding of what happened. Allow the other person to share their insights and their perspectives. The person corrected is more likely to listen and follow through if they feel engaged as part of the solution, instead of being singled out as part of the problem.

Here is an example of how the F.I.X. Correction Technique works.

You cannot find new client entries in the company database. You asked to meet with the person who is entering the content.

You	**F** – Find out what happened by asking questions first.
	Good morning Charlie. I am unable to find any of our clients entered during this quarter. How are the company names listed?
Them	Customers and prospective clients are entered alphabetically by the company contact's last name.
You	**I** – Inform about expectations.
	I see. Since the individual may get promoted, relocated, or leave that company, let's list all clients and prospects alphabetically by company name.
You	**X** – Examine solutions by asking questions.
	What is the best way to update all entries since the last 30 days?

In this example, the person corrected may never recognize this discussion as a correction. This is the beauty of the F.I.X. Correction Technique. By addressing an issue in this capacity, you can boost the other person's accountability and increase the likelihood of correcting an issue only once.

Fire Terms

Words or expressions we perceive as negative can cause others to become defensive. When we become defensive, our temperatures can rise causing us to get hot or "lose our cool!" This is why I call the following words and expressions, Fire Terms. You should modify Fire Terms to keep communication cool.

Let's start with one of the most popular Fire Terms, **"But."** The "but" is grammatically a conjunction. "But" is supposed to join two subordinate clauses. This is the rule of grammar. When it comes to communication, the word "but" does not join, it separates.

For example, if you said the following to someone, *"I like your idea, **but** it costs too much."* What will be the takeaway message retained by the other person? They will feel as if their idea was negated. They may also feel as if there are no next steps or progressions on their idea. A person who feels their ideas are unappreciated may also be reluctant to share future suggestions.

Here is the alternative, replace "but" with a solution-oriented question. For example, *"I like your idea. What can we do to ensure we conduct this plan within our budget?"* Notice in this version, the Fire Term, "but" is omitted. Since the person never hears the Fire Term, their emotional state stays calm. Also, by asking them a question, it can generate future discussion. Even if their idea does not have merit, it can develop their professional and personal maturation to become better decision makers. It also keeps you from looking like a pessimist who can only shoot down ideas instead of building up people.

Another Fire Term is **"You."** This Fire Term can be accusatory. For example, if someone said, **"You** told me it would be ready." Hearing this said to them, a person may feel accused and become defensive. The alternative is to replace the Fire Term **"you"** with the pronoun **"I."** For example, *"I was told it would be ready today."* By replacing the Fire Term with "I," the emphasis of defensiveness is off of the other person.

Another Fire Term is the word, **"Try."** This Fire Term may sound innocent. The intent of using this word may be an attempt to show effort and concern. Some may disregard the good intention and associate this word with the lack of effort and account-ability. The solution is to replace this Fire Term with specific in-formation about what you know you can personally do. Avoid overpromising beyond your control. For example, avoid saying, *"They will call you back by Tuesday."* You may be unable to control what someone can do. Instead, say what you know you can do, *"I will replace the order with the correct shipping address. Our shipping policy is five calendar days. By August 10, I will email you a status update."* Regardless of what happens, you can still do everything you said you could do.

"Why" is another Fire Term, that can make people defensive. Why may be a neutral question in the attempt to ascertain more information. Depending on a person's sensitivity, they may be fine with being asked this Fire Term. Others may find the word accusatory and challenging their thought process. The alternative is to ask any of the following:

- What led to this decision?
- What are the reasons?
- How was this outcome determined?
- What information was provided?
- How was the result concluded?

By keeping the questions neutral, it increases the likelihood you will get a non-defensive answer. Other Fire Terms include:

- Always - exaggeration
- ASAP - demanding without being realistic
- Basically - indecisive without acceptance
- End of business -vague, requiring a guess on completion time
- I didn't know - passive without accountability
- I guess – wavering, needing additional validation

138

- If you say so - doubtful of, remaining in denial
- In a minute- dismissive about your time and expediency
- It is what it is- disregard of continual discussion
- No problem - indicator of perceived intrusion
- Sure - passive aggressive and reluctance to confirm
- That is not my job -lacking accountability or ownership to resolve
- Whatever - immature and lack of acceptance of new information

There are some universal words of profanity and words of understood insensitivity. The Fire Terms are not those types of verbiages that carry the consistent negative connotations. The Fire Terms can be innocent words which can be considered detrimental based on the context of the conversation. During your next opportunity to reply, keep communication high and keep defensives low.

The Five Replies

Responding effectively to others is essential to improving communication. We may have good intentions, but with a poor response choice, it can detour the conversation to an unintended route. Now that you know the alternatives to the Fire Terms let's examine the Five Replies.

It is important to note, out of these five, there is no perfect or better type of reply. Each of the Five Replies will generate a different response. When striving to be an effective communicator as it relates to mastering the Five Replies, I recommend you do the following three things:

1. Understand the purpose for each of the Five Replies.
2. Know where you want the conversation to navigate.
3. Ask the appropriate Reply that results in that direction.

Lead Out Loud!

The Five Replies

Five Replies	Purpose	Examples
1. **Align**	Relate	I understand. I know how you feel.
2. **Critique**	Reprimand	This is a mistake. I would not have done it that way.
3. **Ask**	Inquire	How did this occur?
4. **Tell**	Instruct	Email the agenda before conducting the meeting.
5. **Bounce**	Acknowledge	It can be tough when you feel unappreciated.

1. Align

An Align Response is best when wanting to connect emotionally. This approach can be effective when you want to let the other person know you are considerate of their feelings and you want them to know you are cognizant of what they are experiencing. The Align Reply is one of the most common replies. If overused or mistimed, it can lose its validity. Strive to be conscious of how often you use this reply. Remain aware of how much you are truly in alignment with the other person. Early in my career, I made the mistake of incorrectly using an Align Response.

I was conducting research-oriented interviews. My goal was to listen to how successful people overcame challenges. I had the honor of interviewing a paraplegic businesses owner named Phillip. In his youth, Phillip was an All-American swimmer with aspirations of being an Olympian. Although he lost the use of both of his legs and confined to a wheelchair, he was still an avid swimmer. I asked him, "Phillip, how challenging has it been to maintain your independent lifestyle since the accident?" Philip shared that he felt he was just as active as he has always been. He continued to share that his biggest challenge was not his adjustments to the world. As an independent and strong will person, Philip told me it was difficult for him to adjust to his family and friends assuming he was now helpless. Phillip said he had to curb his frustrations when those closest to him were amazed that he continued participating in and even winning swimming competitions. I detoured a congenial conversation into a disastrous abyss! To relate to Phillip, I foolishly replied with, "I totally understand Phillip. I am an independent person too. I had knee surgery playing high school football. I could not walk for a few days. I know just how you feel." Phillips face changed from a relaxed smile to a disgruntled snarl. He then said to me, "When this interview is over, you will walk out of this room. I will never walk again. You have no idea how that feels."

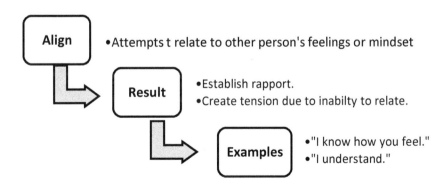

Align
•Attempts t relate to other person's feelings or mindset

Result
•Establish rapport.
•Create tension due to inabilty to relate.

Examples
•"I know how you feel."
•"I understand."

2. Critique

A Critique Response works best when you want to show clear disapproval. There can be times you just want to say exactly what you dislike without using your mental filter. Critique Replies are not problem-solving replies. When using a Critique Reply, you are not trying to understand, relate, or resolve; you are just pointing out a negative. Be mindful; if you overuse the Critique Response, you run the risk of being judged as overly critical and pessimistic. Critique replies can be effective depending on the rapport.

> When I was a child, I was fascinated by my aunt's new stove top and oven. As soon as you would turn the knob to the on position, the burners on top of the stove would illuminate. As soon as you would turn the knob to the off position, the burner would go dim. I was tempted to touch it! My aunt consistently reminded me to stay away from the burners after she had used them. She told me that even though the burner's light was dimmed, the burner was still hot. I assumed she was wrong because if the burner does not look hot, how can it be hot!

> One evening my aunt had cleaned her kitchen after dinner. As she left, my temptation got the best of me. I waited until the burners on the stove went from red to black. I snuck into the kitchen and placed both hands on the burner! When I yelped in pain, my Aunt dashed into the kitchen and nursed my blistered hands. Fortunately, I did not have any serious damage but man, did it hurt! Till this day, the only thing she ever said to me about my mistake was, a single Critique Reply, "I bet you won't be dumb enough to do that again." (She was right☺).

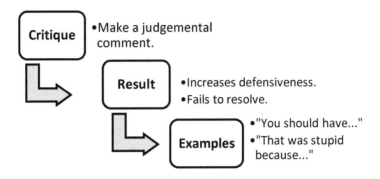

3. Ask

An Ask Reply follows the guidelines of questions in Chapter 4. Whether you use one of the four question techniques:

1. Open

2. Closed

3. Clarity

4. Connector

Remember to follow the six rules of questions as they apply to the Ask Replies:

1. Identify - Know which of the four types of questions you want to ask.

2. Condense - Ask only one question at a time.

3. Pause – Avoid interrupting.

4. Abbreviate - Keep questions short.

5. Clarify - Remove double negatives.

6. Qualify - Put supportive information upfront.

Use Ask Replies when you may be unsure of what to say. Ask Replies work great for continuing the conversation. As a solution-focused person, I use Ask Replies to prevent me from offering solutions prematurely.

My first college job was at Taco Bell. I was considered for a promotion. The supervisor asked me to manage the store during our busiest time of the day, which was the lunch hour. I saw this as an opportunity to demonstrate my leadership skills and earn that promotion. During the lunch rush, a large order came in at once. I became overwhelmed and made mistakes. I accidentally put too many onions on the tacos. I spilled red sauce into a box of nachos. I left off too much cheese on the tostadas and put too many beans in the burritos.

A customer came up to the counter holding a Taco Supreme (a taco with sour cream, lettuce, cheese, and tomatoes). They said, "This is not what I ordered." Although his taco looked perfect to me, I took it from his hand and made him two more Taco Supremes. I was meticulous about doing both perfectly. I was even going to give him an extra Taco Supreme to make up for my blunder. As I constructed his new order, the line at the drive-through and front register got longer. I gave the customer three new Taco Supremes. He became even angrier. "Look, young man, that's not my order!" I then threw all three Taco Supremes in the trash. After giving the customer a voucher for a free meal, I began to explain the ingredients of a Taco Supreme. He and I then debated about how to make tacos!

My supervisor calmly walked between the customer and me. My supervisor said, "Our apologies. What is your order?" The customer magically calmed down. They said, "I ordered two Taco Supremes with sour cream on the side. My wife is allergic to sour cream, but

I still like it. Your employee here keeps putting sour cream on top of my wife's tacos!" As I looked at the menu register, I could see the order was entered as Two Taco Supremes (Side-SC). The (Side-SC) meant, a side of sour cream. I was in such a rush to do a good job; I skipped the process, didn't listen well, and did not look up at the order board. In about two minutes, I threw away three tacos, gave away money for free food, held up the drive-through, and ticked off what I found out later was a nice man.

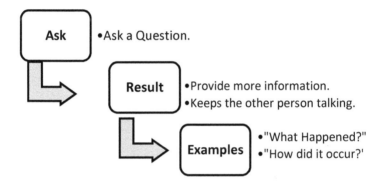

Use Ask Replies to get more information.
The best decisions are informed decisions.

4. Tell

Use Tell Replies when you want an action implemented. Tell Replies are not designed for discussion or inquisition. Tell Replies are mandates or recommendations when a next step or a specific course of action is needed. Be careful overusing Tell Replies, or you can run the risk of seeming dictatorial. Also, be sure to do your due diligence before delegating and dictating to others.

While serving as an investor for a co-operative grocery store, our committee deliberated on whether to serve alcohol and tobacco products in our stores. Half of the committee shared research stating that we could lose community support if we promote poor health habits that contribute to illness in the community. The other half of the committee shared research stating co-ops that fit our profile generated most of their revenue from beer and cigarettes. A solution was nowhere in sight. I used a Tell Reply by stating, "Compare sales for two weeks. Calculate revenue for week one offering alcohol and tobacco. Then calculate revenue for week two without offering alcohol and tobacco. If revenue is most important, trust your customers and profit to decide."

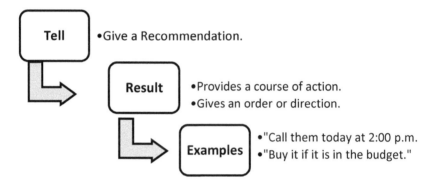

5. Bounce

Use Bounce Replies when you want to remain neutral in discussions. Bounce Replies enable you to stay engaged in the conversation without committing to a side, aggravating the speaker, or telling them what to think or how to feel. A Bounce Reply tells the other person you are still listening, but you are remaining a catcher of the conversation rather than a content contributor. Using Bounce Replies can be challenging if you are opinionated about the topic or care about the person. Bounce Replies require listening, discipline, and restraint.

A friend was turned down for a job for which she felt she was perfect. She suspected the hiring manager's decision to deny her employment was due to a personal dislike rather than her professional accolades. When she vented to me, I was aware of her impressive career accomplishments and her prestigious education. Being aware of how she could exaggerate her importance, I knew she could seem pretentious to others. I got the sense she wanted me to side with her. I allowed her to share her insights without over committing a perspective due to my limited information. I used the following Bounce Replies: "It sounds like you feel this job was a perfect fit for you!" and "It can be tough to be turned down for a job for reasons beyond your control."

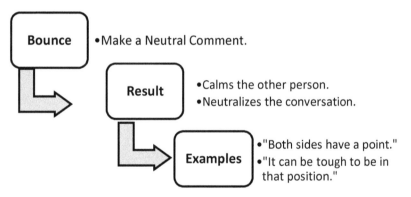

Bounce • Make a Neutral Comment.

Result
• Calms the other person.
• Neutralizes the conversation.

Examples
• "Both sides have a point."
• "It can be tough to be in that position."

Showing Appreciation

Another component to reducing defensiveness is to show value to others. Although we have varying personalities, we all want to be respected and appreciated. One of the best ways reduce conflicts and show appreciation is to give compliments. One might wonder why I would include something as euphoric as how to give compliments in a chapter that addresses the solution of conflicts.

Consider the health of your body. If you exercise daily, eat fruits as snacks, and have freshly cooked vegetables at every meal; you may be able to indulge once or twice a month. If a person was unaware of your daily health commitment and only saw how you eat on your "cheat" day, they may assume your junk food day is your normal. However, you and your body know differently. Since you invested in the commitment to put goodness into your body, your health system is better equipped to counteract any unhealthiness you put into your body.

Considering this analogy, if you continually tell people how much they are valued and appreciated, you invest in their emotional health. When you have to do the inevitable with people, such as give a correction or say something that could cause conflicts, the more you have invested time in building rapport, the more receptive they can be to constructive criticism.

W.O.W. Compliment Technique

The W.O.W. Compliment technique addresses one of our most basic needs of being shown appreciation. The W.O.W. Compliment serves two purposes:

1. Show appreciation to others.

2. Get repeated positive behavior.

Three Steps of the W.O.W. Compliment

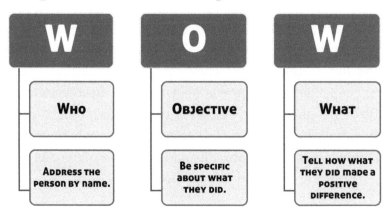

148

These are called W.O.W. Compliments because you want the compliment to be so heartfelt and so personally specific, that when the other person receives the compliment from you, they say, "Wow!". W.O.W. Compliments require more thought than traditional compliments. W.O.W. Compliments take more time to give than traditional compliments.

Traditional Compliment	W.O.W. Compliment
Thanks for your help.	Becky, thank you for organizing the account folders by date and by name. This helps us follow up faster with our customers and prevent mistakes.
I appreciate all you do.	Cedric, thank you for arriving early to our programs. When you check all the equipment and arrange the seating, it enables us to conduct our programs with greater confidence.

Caution in overusing W.O.W. Compliments. These types of compliments work best when the person has done something special or extraordinary. If you are giving W.O.W. Compliments to the same person, ten times a day, it may get weird. Avoid giving compliments that sound like, *"Thank you, Charles, for opening the door for me. You enabled me to enter the room without using my hands."*

Lead Out Loud!

CHAPTER CHALLENGE

During your next conflict:
- Replace statements of feeling with facts.
- Avoid terms that make others defensive.
- Choose the response to get the desired results.
- Show appreciation by complementing effectively.

Conclusion

What are you doing to become a better communicator? What are you doing to become a better person? How is what you are doing, going to make the people around you better?

This dapper gentleman pictured below is my grandfather, Johnny Bae Johnson. My grandparents had seven girls and no boys. I love hearing my grandfather tell stories of his organizational system coordinating bath time between nine people — one male and eight females — in the same house with only one bathroom! Now, my mother and all six of my aunts own homes with at least two bathrooms!

My grandfather is regarded as a man with wisdom, wit, and charisma. His suaveness seems to catapult off this image!

Remember these words from my grandfather, "There are two types of people in the world, those with the personality that can brighten a room just by walking in, and those with the personality that can brighten a room just by walking out!"

Amplify your life to amplify the lives of others.

You can receive a FREE newsletter, special rates, and other updates at www.communicationvip.com

Remember to E-mail Vincent and claim
your digital copy at Vincent@CommunicationVIP.com

Please take a moment to leave a review of Lead Out Loud on Amazon.com. Thank you.

Lead Out Loud Tools

Lead Out Loud!

S

T

W